S0-AIU-218

CEILING UNLIMITED

CEILING UNLIMITED

The story of
NORTH CENTRAL AIRLINES

By Robert J. Serling

Walsworth Publishing Company
Marceline, Missouri

Photograph on inside front cover by Colonel Forest J. Sorenson, Minnesota Air National Guard (ret). Photograph on inside back cover by Captain Robert L. Smith, North Central Airlines.

Copyright 1973 by Walsworth Publishing Company, Inc. All rights reserved. Printed in the United States of America.

LIBRARY OF CONGRESS CATALOG CARD NUMBER: 73-90730

Foreword

This is the story of an airline and its first twenty-five years. It could be told in just two columns of statistics:

	1948	1972
Plane miles flown	794,668	29,199,983
Passengers carried	11,398	4,318,643
Air cargo (pounds)	345,535	86,729,211
Employees	152	3,250
Cities served	23	91
Route miles	1,080	9,916
Total revenues	$703,724	$120,627,442
Net profit (loss)	$(128,044)	$7,535,878

It would be easy to produce similar statistics for any airline; this particular one has been part of aviation's tremendous progress, not an exclusive holder of a franchise to grow. But progress is not the full story. No set of cold figures can reflect how humble the beginning, how tough the uphill climb. No slickly-written annual report can do more than hint at the political brawling, the bitter feuds that are part of corporate successes and failures. No financial box score can relate the real exploits of the heroes and the villains, the generals and the spear carriers.

An airline is a corporate entity, but it also is the living, breathing sum of all the human parts that went into it. It is a machine—from the whirling, clicking computers to the great silver birds that fly its routes—but it also mirrors the skills and loyalties and dreams of those who stand behind the machines.

This is the story of one airline, North Central. In many ways, it could be the story of every airline—the giants like United and TWA; the smaller trunks like Western and Continental; or the growing regionals like Allegheny, Piedmont and Frontier. All the nation's airlines have one thing in common: they started with virtually nothing, and today they form the world's finest air transportation system.

North Central is part of that history and a part of that system. But it has its own story—a unique one. The story of the men who were its midwives even though they knew nothing about aviation. The story of a man who saved it from destruction. The story of the pilots, flight attendants, station managers, dispatchers, mechanics, agents, salesmen, secretaries, schedulers and executives who fused a human personality into the technological robot that is an air carrier.

This is *their* history of North Central. They wrote it; what you are about to read merely records their deeds.

Robert J. Serling

Potomac, Maryland
May 15, 1973

To the men and women of North Central
who for twenty-five years have proved
that "Good people make an airline great"

Contents

CHAPTER ONE

Taxi

The letter was dated June 21, 1944; it was addressed to Richard Milbauer—a prominent merchant in the small Wisconsin community of Clintonville—and the postmark was Washington, D.C.

Dear Dick:

I don't know whether you have missed me or not, but I've been down here with FDR for the past week trying to convince the folks that we need a franchise for our airline. Our application will be filed tomorrow, and there is to be a prehearing conference next Tuesday. The final hearing will be about sixty days from now and involves a great deal of research in order to establish that there is a need for air transportation in each of the communities to be served.

We are proposing to run one route from Chicago to Duluth and another route from Marquette, Michigan, down through Green Bay and across the state to La Crosse, Rochester and St. Paul. If we get all that we ask for, we will have a real airline using Clintonville as the terminal junction for both routes.

I expect to be home in a week or so and will be anxious to have an opportunity to tell you more about it.

> Very truly yours,
> The Four Wheel Drive Auto Co.
> *Francis M. Higgins*
> Advertising Manager

If Francis Higgins had known what lay ahead, he probably would have written Milbauer something along the lines of "Dear Dick: To hell with it." Fortunately for the embryonic airline, he was an optimist—and also a promoter.

Francis M. Higgins served as Wisconsin Central's first President from its incorporation in 1944 to 1952.

By his own admission, Higgins knew pitifully little about aviation. He was heading the safari into the jungles of Washington mostly because nobody else at The Four Wheel Drive Auto Company (FWD) knew much about aviation either. FWD itself had started out in Clintonville in 1910 with vital patents on a four-wheel-drive transmission, and had become one of the country's major manufacturers of heavy-duty trucks.

In the early days, FWD utilized the excellent rail facilities between Clintonville and such cities as Chicago and Milwaukee. But rail service, which at one time amounted to twenty schedules a day serving Clintonville, declined steadily as northern Wisconsin's logging industry slumped. By 1937, Clintonville was being visited by a single north-south freight train, and if passengers needed transportation, they had to ride in the caboose.

It was an impossible situation for fast-growing FWD. Roads were poor, bus service abysmally slow, and it was obvious that air transportation was the only answer. Clintonville had an airport of sorts—a forty-acre field whimsically designated "airport" by the Civil Aeronautics Authority provided that a windsock be installed and the grass mowed along the runway during the summer.

By 1939, FWD President Walter A. Olen took drastic action. He traded a company truck even-up for a used four-place Waco biplane and called in Higgins, his advertising manager.

"We got an airplane, but Lindbergh himself couldn't use that field," he told Higgins. "See if you can do something about getting it improved."

Higgins did. He talked officials in Waupaca County and Clintonville into expanding the airport to 140 acres—with FWD's financial support. Two new landing strips were built and so was a hangar—out of used metal. The Waco started flying FWD officials to Chicago two or three times a week, and the service proved so popular that Olen shelled out $25,000 for a Howard monoplane.

Even the two-plane "airline" turned out to be inadequate, for other Clintonville businessmen were hooking rides to Chicago on a space-available basis. Early in 1944, it occurred to Olen that passenger business was promising enough to stop giving free rides. He decided to incorporate the airline and charge for its services.

On May 15, 1944, the legal papers were signed, and Wisconsin Central Airlines was born.

The three incorporators were Olen, Higgins, and Herbert S. Foth, member of a Green Bay engineering firm which had handled airport construction projects. Because of this experience, Foth was considered by Olen and Higgins to be something of an "authority" on aviation. The Articles of Incorporation state that the capital stock in the new company "shall be $50,000, divided into 5,000 shares." FWD acquired 52 percent of

To carry company officials between Chicago and Clintonville, Wisconsin, The Four Wheel Drive Auto Company traded a truck for a four-place Waco biplane in 1939.

the airline's stock, with Clintonville businessmen holding the remaining shares.

The new company's first stockholders' meeting was held on May 15 at 7:30 p.m. in the offices of FWD. The stockholders approved the Bylaws of the new corporation and elected eight directors, hand-picked by Olen because of their interest in promoting airline service to the community.

Following this, the directors held their first meeting. The minutes show that "E. Gehrke nominated F. M. Higgins for the office of President, and there being no further nominations, F. M. Higgins was declared elected."

The other officers named at this meeting were Foth as Vice President; Arthur E. Schwandt, an FWD accountant, as Secretary; and Bernard O. Stieg, son of the local banker, as Treasurer. All of the officers were to serve without compensation.

Olen had ordered Higgins to keep an eye on the aircraft operation from the time the Waco was acquired, which he did with alacrity. As the prime mover in the original local airport improvement, Higgins had been named Chairman of the Clintonville Chamber of Commerce Aviation Committee. Overseeing the more-or-less regular air service fascinated him. When FWD decided to go into the airline business seriously, Higgins was the logical choice for field commander.

The new president of Wisconsin Central Airlines was a burly, ebullient, likeable man of 43 with shaggy hair crowning a face that could have been

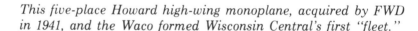

This five-place Howard high-wing monoplane, acquired by FWD in 1941, and the Waco formed Wisconsin Central's first "fleet."

Walter A. Olen, President of The Four Wheel Drive Auto Company, was one of the three incorporators of Wisconsin Central in 1944, along with Francis Higgins and Herbert Foth.

Herbert S. Foth, one of Wisconsin Central's three incorporators, was named Vice President at the company's first directors' meeting in 1944.

Arthur E. Schwandt, FWD accountant, was elected Secretary of Wisconsin Central at the first directors' meeting.

hewed out of solid granite. He looked like a professional football lineman, although fate had decreed he could never be an athlete. At the age of seven, Higgins was stricken with polio that left him with a decided limp. It was typical of him that he always joked about it, telling everyone, "I just have a distinctive walk."

At FWD, Higgins was highly regarded—being in charge of advertising and public relations. He performed his tasks with humor, patience and a knack for salesmanship, all of which qualities he needed when he became president of the airline. For FWD had no intention of keeping Wisconsin Central a private carrier basically serving the needs of FWD and Clintonville with a couple of tiny aircraft.

For many years, Olen had a deep interest and had been active in promoting all forms of transportation. He visualized and strongly advocated a network of local airlines "to provide the benefits of air transportation to the nation's smaller communities."

In 1943, the Civil Aeronautics Board had announced an investigation to determine the feasibility of "feeder" air service. As a result of this investigation, it was decided that hearings would be held to select qualified applicants to receive certificates for providing regional scheduled service to smaller cities—those not on the routes of the trunk carriers or served at such a loss that the trunks were anxious to abandon them.

Olen had heard of the CAB program, and in June of 1944, one month after the company was formed, he dispatched Higgins to Washington with instructions to "get one of those new airline franchises."

Higgins, however, was not the only one pounding on various government doors. By the time the hearings were underway to designate the new airline operators, some 1,600 parties had filed applications or otherwise indicated an interest in obtaining a franchise. In fact, the area in which Wisconsin Central proposed to operate had no less than thirty-four applicants, an obstacle which didn't faze Higgins one bit.

Wisconsin Central's application for Federal certification had been composed carefully, with due emphasis on FWD's financial stability and the fact that Wisconsin Central was already an operating airline—which may have been stretching the truth slightly. After one week in Washington, Higgins sat down in his hotel room and wrote to the FWD and Clintonville backers. One such letter went to Max Stieg, President of the Dairyman's State Bank, and it bears quoting because it indicates that, with all his natural enthusiasm and confidence, Higgins himself had been jarred by the complications of the certification process.

Dear Max:

I have been in Washington for the past week in connection with filing our application for a franchise for the airline. While actual preparation of the application is quite simple, the airlines are very carefully regulated, and a great deal of research is necessary in order to prepare oneself for the questions that are to be asked at the prehearing conference to be held here June 27. We have hired a firm of attorneys here to handle the matter which is very specialized and must be handled in a very careful manner.

Yesterday we had an opportunity to have an interview with the examiner who is to hear the thirty-four cases for franchises in the Wisconsin area. He looked over our application and said it was in perfect order. Judging from past experience, the final hearings will be about sixty days after the preliminary hearing so we are very opportune in filing at this time. Otherwise, there might have been a delay of as much as two years in hearing our case . . .

Best regards,
Francis Higgins

The attorneys mentioned in the Stieg letter were Roberts & McInnis, a well-known law firm specializing in transportation and communications cases. Higgins was not acquainted with any lawyers in Washington so he had asked the advice of FWD's representative there who suggested Roberts & McInnis. Higgins met with the head of the firm, William A. Roberts, who had just returned from service in World War II and was intrigued with the plans to set up a new airline.

Actually, Higgins was being overly optimistic in boasting about saving two years by filing in the middle of 1944. Certification did not come for another two and a half years.

As Wisconsin Central's case before the CAB progressed through the many procedural steps, the company continued to provide some service with the Howard and Waco aircraft which had been purchased from FWD in October 1945 for $8,000. This service was under the general managership of Percy V. Chaffee, the fixed base operator at the Clintonville Airport. In January 1946, the directors accepted Chaffee's resignation from the airline, and Higgins was authorized to engage James J. Mulva, an FWD employee, as General Manager.

During this time, the company was constructing a small hangar at the Clintonville airport to serve as its headquarters. The project, being supervised by Foth, was encountering considerable delay due to a lack of funds, as well as the shortage of steel and other building materials. After the walls had been erected, disaster struck in the form of a violent storm which flattened the partially completed building.

Fortunately, one of the directors, G. F. (Joe) DeCoursin, had the uncanny foresight to take out insurance on the building just the day before the storm. The money received from the insurance settlement enabled the company to proceed once more with the project.

DeCoursin, who was a production supervisor with FWD, had been selected to serve on the Board because Olen regarded him as a "bright young man." His action in insuring the building certainly justified Olen's opinion of him. However, DeCoursin was destined to play a significantly more important role in the company's development in the years to come.

The company received another staggering blow just a month later, in March 1946. The CAB examiner in the North Central Area Investigation

Wisconsin Central Airlines' main base hangar, erected at the Clintonville Airport in 1945, was the company's first home.

G. F. DeCoursin, FWD employee, was one of Wisconsin Central's eight original directors.

issued his report and recommended that Wisconsin Central should not be selected to operate an airline.

The examiner stated that, "if Wisconsin Central obtained a certificate, FWD would be placed in a position in which its natural tendencies would be to operate the airline for its own interest rather than that of the public." As evidence of this, he pointed out that FWD had acquired control of a common motor carrier by truck, the Clintonville Transfer Line, in order to obtain improved freight transportation service. Accordingly, the examiner recommended that the CAB find that "Wisconsin Central is not fit, willing, and able to perform its proposed service."

Undaunted by this development, Higgins continued his efforts to raise capital through stock sales and bank borrowing. He and the other directors also realized the importance of improving Wisconsin Central's image in the eyes of the CAB. To do this, it was decided that the company should conduct a scheduled intrastate operation.

After the examiner's recommendation, the Howard aircraft was sold, and two five-passenger, twin-engine Cessnas were acquired. On April 4, a regularly scheduled operation was inaugurated providing flights five days a week to Madison, Milwaukee, Clintonville, Wausau, Rhinelander, and Superior, Wisconsin.

This intrastate service with the twin Cessnas was notable primarily because it accelerated the drain on the company's meager capital. At a directors' meeting in August, Treasurer Stieg presented a statement to the

Board showing the approximate financial position of the company as "a cash deficit of $14,171." On November 1, the intrastate operation was terminated, and Mulva resigned as General Manager of the company.

The CAB's delay in issuing its final decision in the North Central Area Investigation was proving disastrous to the company. Higgins had expected the CAB order before the end of the summer. In fact, A. L. (Al) Wheeler, the attorney with Roberts & McInnis who was handling the Wisconsin Central case, advised him in July that the order might be forthcoming within ten days.

Early in December, even the usually cheerful Higgins was discouraged. He confided to DeCoursin that the airline was "at the end of its rope." The company had no money, only two employees remained, the intrastate operation had been suspended, the examiner's recommendation was unfavorable, and it appeared that the CAB decision might be delayed indefinitely. He told DeCoursin, "It will take a miracle to keep us from going under."

On the last day of the year, December 31, 1946, the miracle happened. The CAB issued its final decision in the case and, to the surprise of almost everyone, reversed the examiner's recommendation by selecting Wisconsin Central over all other regional applicants to become a certificated airline.

These twin-engine, five-place Cessna UC-78s, parked at the Clintonville Airport, replaced the original Waco and Howard aircraft and were used by Wisconsin Central in its charter and intrastate operation from 1945 to 1947.

The CAB order was beyond Higgins' wildest dreams. It authorized the company to operate approximately 1,400 route miles serving forty-three cities via such metropolitan terminals as Chicago, Milwaukee, Green Bay, Minneapolis/St. Paul and Duluth/Superior.

There was great joy in Clintonville that New Year's Eve, and Higgins was not the only one to prophesy that the small city would become one of the major transportation hubs in the Midwest.

Once more, if he had been able to visualize the obstacles that lay ahead, Higgins might have abandoned the entire project. However, as a supreme optimist, he felt that the award of the certificate had solved most of the airline's problems. Actually, some of the most difficult times were to come in the next year.

The CAB order designating Wisconsin Central to receive a temporary certificate contained a jolting provision: FWD could own no part of the new airline. This meant that FWD's stock in Wisconsin Central must all be sold to private investors. The financial problem seemed overwhelming. Not only did the company have to raise hundreds of thousands of dollars to get the airline operation started, but it had to find buyers for the FWD stock to comply with the CAB order.

Higgins kept reading and rereading the CAB decision. The pride he felt was diluted considerably by the problems he faced. Wisconsin Central had no airplanes, totally inadequate facilities in a small town of less than 5,000 persons, only a few employees, and virtually no money.

In this crucial period when he was frantically trying to raise capital, Higgins was also looking around for experienced airline personnel. On the recommendation of Roberts, he hired Colonel A. Irvine Pett, a highly decorated Air Force officer, to head up flight operations and maintenance. What he needed in particular, however, was a right-hand man who knew intimately the problems of running an airline. Again he asked Roberts to recommend someone.

Roberts pondered the request.

"There's one guy in the executive offices at TWA," the lawyer said finally. "He helped set up TWA's international routes and testifies for them in CAB cases. He seems to be very able and has done some work for our firm as a consultant on aviation matters. In fact, he assisted in preparing the exhibits for your case. Awfully young, though—he's just in his twenties."

"I don't care if he wears rompers," Higgins rasped, "so long as he knows this business. What's his name, and where can I contact him?"

"His name's Hal Carr," Roberts replied, "and he's right here in Washington."

A meeting between Higgins and Carr was arranged quickly. Higgins liked the younger man instinctively and immediately. The feeling was mutual. Only twenty-five years old, twenty years junior to Higgins, Carr had been handed major responsibilities in TWA's mushrooming postwar expansion, and he was fast becoming an expert in airline development.

Hal N. Carr had graduated from Texas A&M University and joined TWA as a research analyst at their general offices in Kansas City after serving in the Army during World War II. At TWA Carr was considered bright, personable and clearly a comer. He had been promoted rapidly and was now Assistant Director of Route Development on the staff of TWA's Chairman of the Board in Washington.

The upshot of the meeting was Higgins' offer to Carr of the position of Vice President-Traffic at a salary somewhat below what he was making at TWA. Carr accepted after Higgins slightly upped his first offer although the youthful TWA official had considerable reservations as to whether the fledgling airline would ever get off the ground.

"It was an exciting challenge," he later recalled. "I figured I was getting in at the very beginning of a new air transportation concept. In aviation terminology, it was a ceiling and visibility unlimited situation."

Carr arrived in Clintonville in the middle of a May snowstorm, but fortunately his reception by FWD and Clintonville people was warmer, and he quickly went to work organizing the almost non-existent airline.

Wisconsin Central flew this Cessna UC-78 in its 1947 intrastate operation. Pilot Maury Murray (left) and his four passengers filled the aircraft to capacity.

Hal N. Carr joined Wisconsin Central in 1947 as Vice President-Traffic.

The first priority, of course, was to raise money. Carr soon found himself to be the newly-named "Assistant Fund Raiser". Higgins and Carr figured they would need nearly $1 million in capital to start operations. Raising this amount, in addition to selling FWD's stock, would be harder than mining coal with a nail file.

The entire airline industry was going through a severe postwar recession. Domestic airline stock which had been averaging $37.02 a share in 1945 was down to $12.87 the following year, and dropped to $8.42 in 1947—just at the time Higgins and Carr faced their horrendous selling task.

No two political candidates ever beat the bushes and scoured the grass roots like this pair of would-be airline executives. They talked to housewives, farmers, merchants, barbers, plumbers, carpenters and anyone else who would listen to them. One night they were in Stevens Point, Wisconsin, after a day in which they had failed to sell a single share. Higgins suggested that they go to a local night spot to drown their disappointments. Carr was at the bar when he noticed Higgins was no longer with him.

A quick inspection located the President of Wisconsin Central Airlines. Higgins was standing at the end of a long line of men near the bar, frantically signing them up for stock. He had hit a minor jackpot—a grocers' convention was in Stevens Point, and like most happy conventioneers, they would have bought shares in the Brooklyn Bridge.

Higgins did so well that he ran out of regular forms and was writing temporary stock subscriptions on paper napkins.

Such windfalls, however, were infrequent. Higgins was many thousands of dollars short of even the most modest goals—and desperate—when Loewi & Co., a Milwaukee investment firm, agreed to try to form an underwriting group to sell a $400,000 stock issue. The transaction, which dragged on for months, finally netted Wisconsin Central about $350,000—only a third of what was supposed to be the minimum needed. Higgins and Carr decided to take a chance and go with the proverbial shoestring.

A shoestring was about all they had. Carr warned Higgins that airport rentals and landing fees alone might eat up a sizeable chunk of their slim capital.

Francis Higgins (right), airline President, signed up stock subscribers on paper napkins after he ran out of regular forms. At left is Ralph (Stub) Roberts.

"Landing fees?" Higgins groaned. "How much?"

Carr indicated these might amount to several thousand dollars a month.

"Let's hit the road again," Higgins decreed.

They visited every stop on the proposed system. In each city, they told officials the truth: Wisconsin Central couldn't operate without some indirect financial help in the form of temporarily waived landing fees. Either that or no air service, was their frank message. The result was better than expected. The smaller cities agreed to set the landing fees at the unheard of price of one dollar for the first year of operation. They got a further bonus when the big terminal points, like Chicago and Milwaukee, substantially reduced landing fees below what the trunks were paying.

Higgins and Carr had to do another sales job involving the thirteen intermediate airports they intended to serve initially. Most of these had sod runways or graded earth, and some of the paved runways were too short to handle transport aircraft. Once more, the cities were told they had to improve airfields that fell below Federal safety standards. Again, the communities agreed to meet minimum requirements.

Lengthening runways constituted the vast bulk of the improvements; no city had enough funds for fancy terminals, or even such taken-for-granted items as runway lights and navigational aids.

President Francis Higgins (left) and Executive Vice President Hal Carr held numerous planning sessions in the airline's pre-operational days.

Among other problems Carr faced was what might charitably be called an inexperienced Board of Directors. Honest, intelligent men with integrity and faith in the future, yes—but with no real knowledge of the agonies inevitable in the launching of an airline.

At the first Board meeting Carr attended after joining the company in the spring, he noticed that at least one member promptly fell asleep. This irked Carr, but not as much as the first order of business. One of the directors rose to propose that all Board members be named vice presidents of Wisconsin Central.

"That's just great," Carr responded. "We have no airplanes, no stations, no ground personnel and no pilots—but we'll have more vice presidents than American Airlines."

After the defeat of this motion, Carr was further stunned by the suggestion of another director who proposed "that the Board authorize the purchase of thirteen Pontiac station wagons to transport passengers to and from our planes."

Carr, well aware of this director's interest in a Pontiac dealership, exploded. The meeting finally ended in an atmosphere smoky with undisguised hostility. Later that day, DeCoursin approached the still-fuming Carr.

"You made a helluva mistake telling the directors they were full of crap," DeCoursin said bluntly.

"Listen and listen carefully," Carr retorted. "I came here to start an airline, and I'm gonna start one if I have to insult everyone who gets in my way with some half-baked scheme!"

He strode away and left DeCoursin looking at his departing figure with new respect.

A short time later, DeCoursin accompanied Carr on a business trip to Washington. The first evening, still wary of each other, they sanctimoniously decided to see a movie for relaxation. However, it was a fraud that neither of them could perpetrate. Halfway through the show, they confessed to their mutual interest in having a drink, adjourned abruptly to the nearest bar, and became the closest of friends.

Carr needed men like DeCoursin as allies. The affable Higgins, who had the personality of an uninhibited puppy, hated to get mad at anyone and squirmed if anyone got mad at him. The usually hectic Board meetings in those critical pre-operational days found the President invariably trying to compromise between the ineptness of some Board members and Carr's steel-cutting recommendations.

Higgins, for example, dreaded one of those proposals. Carr was convinced that Wisconsin Central could not be based in Clintonville. He

16

wanted the headquarters moved to Madison where the airport was more modern and larger facilities were available. DeCoursin still remembers the bitterness Carr generated. Wisconsin Central's roots, bloodlines and soul were in the small town, and as DeCoursin put it, "the heavy hand of Walter Olen was very much in evidence at those early Board meetings."

It was DeCoursin, younger and far more flexible than the other directors, who sided with Carr and eventually swung the Board over. After the decision was made to move and Clintonville seethed with natural resentment, DeCoursin went to Walter Gleason, editor of the local paper, and explained why it was necessary.

"If we don't have bigger quarters," he told Gleason, "the time will come when it will be impossible to operate out of Clintonville. Moving's inevitable, and it's best to do it now before service is started."

Gleason's editorial support helped quell the ill feeling. (Years later on the occasion of the airline's tenth anniversary, the official celebration was held in Clintonville, and an appropriate plaque noting Wisconsin Central's Clintonville origins was given to the city.)

In his efforts to organize the airline, Carr encountered increasing difficulties in his relationship with Pett whom the Board had appointed Vice President-Operations. The two differed sharply in personality and airline philosophy alike. Pett looked upon Carr as too young for his position

Colonel A. I. (Irv) Pett (right) who joined the airline as Vice President of Operations in 1947 is shown at the Clintonville Airport with Wisconsin Central's first Lockheed 10A.

and regarded his directness and devotion to perfection, excessive. Carr considered Pett's methods to be ineffective. Unfortunately for Carr, his position as Vice President-Traffic gave him no official authority to pull rank on the other Vice President.

The sharp differences between the two officers extended to matters of equipment selection, organizational responsibility, and financial priorities. Higgins expressed his concern to the other directors and told them that unless the conflicts were settled promptly, he was afraid the start of operations would be further delayed.

Shortly after this, on December 10, 1947, the Board held a meeting with Pett and Carr in the Clintonville hangar to review their progress in starting service. Carr listened carefully to the report of the Vice President-Operations. Pett emphasized the tremendous problems to be solved before the company would qualify for an air carrier operating certificate from the Civil Aeronautics Authority (the Federal agency responsible for regulating airline safety.) He indicated that before service could be inaugurated, the company would have to acquire and convert additional aircraft, spare engines, propellers and a multitude of other parts, and also conduct an extensive training program for pilots and mechanics. Pett estimated that the Operations Department would require a cash budget of at least $50,000 more to accomplish all this.

Carr observed that the directors were virtually overwhelmed by the magnitude of the tasks that lay ahead. Rather than dwell on the problems in his department, Carr decided to outline the accomplishments.

The minutes of the meeting show Carr reported to the Board that all necessary tariffs had been filed with the CAB and were approved. Proposed schedules had been filed with both the CAB and Post Office Department. The company had been accepted as a member of the Air Transport Association, and an agreement had been entered into with the Railway Express Agency to carry air express. All stations at the cities to be served initially were being equipped; and station personnel, hired and trained. Carr also advised that landing fee and office space agreements had been concluded with all of the cities at very favorable rates. He indicated that the Traffic Department would need only $17,000 to complete its program.

After the meeting was adjourned, the directors got together informally. They decided that to provide Higgins with the managerial muscle they felt he needed and at the same time resolve the difficulties between Carr and Pett, they should officially designate Carr the "Number Two" man in the organization. At their next meeting on January 14, 1948, the directors elected Carr Executive Vice President with complete responsibility for the day-to-day operation of the airline.

Business and civic leaders inspected Wisconsin Central's first Lockheed 10A at the Clintonville base in 1947. To save money, the plane was only painted on one side.

Probably the most important single decision which management had to make at this time was the selection of the type of plane the airline would operate. There was general agreement that the best aircraft available was the Douglas DC-3. Higgins and Carr, only too cognizant of Wisconsin Central's wobbly finances, pointed out to the Board that a used DC-3 in 1947 was selling for more than the plane cost when brand-new. Before settling the matter, the Board also had to turn down another vehement equipment suggestion: one of the directors insisted that the ideal plane for Wisconsin Central's routes was the ancient Ford Tri-Motor. When this proposal was firmly refused, he resigned from the Board in anger.

In truth, Wisconsin Central wound up with a transport plane almost as old as the Ford. It was finally decided to purchase the Lockheed 10A Electra—a ten-passenger aircraft that dated back to 1934. Only the price was right. The six 10As which were eventually acquired averaged $12,000 apiece, compared to about $50,000 that a war-weary DC-3 would have cost.

Carr, who had left TWA when the big carrier was operating four-engine pressurized Constellations, wasn't happy, but the 10A was all Wisconsin Central could afford. Besides, several of the airports to be served did not have adequate runways to accommodate larger planes.

The effervescent Higgins considered the outmoded Lockheed 10A a challenge to his promotional ability. He composed the first news releases and advertisements himself, pointing with pride to the plane's capacity for ten passengers plus baggage, mail and cargo.

"Because of its high overall speed and minimum landing and takeoff requirements," Higgins enthused, "the Electra is considered to be the most

suitable aircraft available today for this type of regional airline service. Many of the major trunklines have used Electras in the past to develop new routes."

Carr could only smile wryly at Higgins' literary ability. The 10A was so obsolete that even Wisconsin Central's new feeder line colleagues considered the plane an aeronautical anachronism. Wisconsin Central, in fact, bought its first two 10As in August of 1947 from another feeder line, Pioneer, which was re-equipping with DC-3s. Later that fall, a third 10A was purchased.

With the acquisition of this modest fleet came the need for airmen to fly the planes. Nineteen pilots were hired, the first being Duane E. Petit, a veteran of sixty-five missions over Europe; his Wisconsin Central seniority started June 7, 1946. Others included Robert Ceronsky, who left United to take a chance with the new airline, and Walter Plew, a former test pilot with Chance-Vought Aircraft. Ralph Parkinson and Arthur Hinke were flying a DC-3 with a Wisconsin intrastate carrier when they decided to go to work for Wisconsin Central—a decision made under the assumption that the new company would also be operating DC-3s. The original pilots, all with military flying backgrounds, reported to Captain Ray Ashley who had joined the airline as Chief Pilot in November 1947.

20

Wisconsin Central's original nineteen pilots on February 24, 1948. From left are Raymond Ashley, Ralph Parkinson, Arthur Hinke, Lloyd Franke, Francis Van Hoof, Alexander (Bill) Banks, Rodney Dixon, Donald Planck, Herbert Splettstoeser, Robert Ceronsky, William Bittner, Charles Nason, Milton Ellyson, Walter Plew, Frederic Kremer, and Earl Barron. Duane (Pete) Petit, Robert Swennes, and John Downing are not shown.

The entire fleet of Wisconsin Central Lockheed 10As when service began in 1948.

*Thomas M. Needham joined
Wisconsin Central in 1947 as
Superintendent of Stations.*

*Captains Pete Petit (left) and Bob Ceronsky peer from a Lockheed
10A cockpit in 1947.*

For key ground personnel, Carr brought in Tom Needham, whom he had known when both were with TWA in Washington. Needham was named Superintendent of Stations and was told to set up Wisconsin Central's ground operations, plus a reservations and communications system—on a budget that wouldn't have financed a good binge. Needham's first question was, "How much can you afford to pay a station manager?"

"Not more than $170 a month," Carr said. "Can you hire good men for that?"

"Sure," Needham said with a lot more outward confidence than he felt inside.

Late in 1947, the company was gradually transferred to Madison. About that time, several of the Clintonville directors, disillusioned by the move from their city, resigned and were replaced with candidates suggested by Loewi & Co. which was insisting on representation on the Board. The new members included Fred V. Gardner, a Milwaukee financial consultant, and Milo Snyder, a Loewi Vice President. Within six months after the relocation in Madison, only two of the original directors were still on the Board—Higgins and DeCoursin.

Loewi & Co. was having a difficult time attempting to form the underwriting group to sell the airline's stock. As one financial writer reported, the Wisconsin Central stock issue seemed to leave the investment community in a "frenzy of indifference."

Contracting for facilities at the Madison airport, Higgins and Carr again succeeded in making very favorable arrangements. With the support and encouragement of Robert Skuldt, Madison airport superintendent and former Air Force pilot, the company was able to negotiate a lease with the City providing for a large hangar to serve as the general office and main operations base, space in the terminal building, and landing fees—for a total of $500 a month.

At the same time, Wisconsin Central received $350-$400 monthly from tenants who sublet space in the hangar. In addition, barracks were set up in one part of the hangar where the newly hired pilots, station managers and mechanics lived while undergoing training.

Although the Madison hangar was substantially larger than the one in Clintonville, it certainly could not be considered the Taj Mahal of airline facilities. It was an old Air Force hangar which had been turned over to the City of Madison at the end of World War II. The roof leaked, the heating plant worked intermittently, and as one employee described it, "The windows were so loose that they hardly slowed down the winter winds." In spite of all this, everyone in the company was grateful, for they at least had a building large enough to house the three Lockheed 10As.

One day Needham went to Carr and complained he had no money to furnish the stations he was supposed to start operating.

"This is some operation you talked me into," he ranted. "Hell, my desk is an empty Coke case."

"Don't complain," Carr replied, thinking of the plush office he had enjoyed at TWA. "Mine's a gas drum."

Higgins and Carr solved one of Needham's problems when the "Missionary Twins" hit the boondocks trail again and convinced the intermediate cities to build their own ticket counters and furnish station space for a rental of just $1 to $2 per square foot annually. But the new Superintendent of Stations was having other troubles.

He managed to hire fifteen subordinates, only five with any previous airline experience. Inasmuch as station managers would have to wear about eight hats, this meant training.

One important job involved weather reporting—a prerequisite for a manager at any airport without a control tower or Weather Bureau

Airport Superintendent Robert B. Skuldt (left) helped the airline acquire this former Air Force hangar (below) at Truax Field in Madison, Wisconsin. The building served as Wisconsin Central's headquarters from 1948 to 1952.

facilities. With the start of service only two months away, Needham discovered that no weather-observing equipment would be available for at least three months. He solved this dilemma by virtually going down on his hands and knees before a Weather Bureau official in Madison, who apparently couldn't stand the sight of a grown man on the verge of tears. The official loaned Needham enough equipment for training purposes and airport installations.

Another Needham discovery involved the unique personality of each newly hired station manager—the ticket agent-salesman-baggage handler-weather observer-cargo clerk-public relations representative—all rolled into one person. Briefly stated, anyone willing to perform these innumerable, diverse chores for $170 a month—and in a winter area that made Siberia resemble Miami Beach—had to be a rugged individualist.

Included among the ground personnel hired was a one-eyed Air Force veteran named Charles Cox. He applied to Wisconsin Central on the recommendation of Pett, who had met Cox in the military. He sent Cox to see Needham, and the superintendent got an early glimpse of Charlie's *modus operandi*.

It seems Needham had hired an applicant from Cleveland to be station manager at Hibbing, Minnesota. The young man was a promising prospect with at least some airline experience. Cox, who was from Hibbing, was offered the post of assistant station manager—a position he considered roughly in the same professional stratum as latrine orderly. The unsuspecting Needham suggested to Cox that he brief his boss-to-be on what to expect in the Northern Minnesota community.

"Glad to," Cox promised, and promptly went into a huddle with the new man.

"What are the schools like in Hibbing?" was the first question. "I've got a couple of youngsters."

"Damned good," Cox assured him. "Of course, we lose a few kids every winter."

"Lose kids?"

"Yeah. It's the weather. Never gets higher than 25 below between October and mid-April. It's easy to lose a kid in a twelve-foot snowbank."

The Clevelander gulped.

"Well," he said hopefully, "at least I suppose it's cheaper to live in Hibbing. I imagine the cost of living is considerably less in a small town."

"Not necessarily," Cox cautioned. "I've lived there most of my life, and a couple of hundred dollars will last you only about ten days—and that's just for basic necessities like food and rent."

His future boss was beginning to pale.

"Those tough winters you mentioned," he ventured. "Do they keep the roads pretty clear? I assume I wouldn't have any trouble getting to the airport."

"Not if you use snowshoes," Cox assured him soberly. "The snow's too deep for plows. But what the hell, you'll really get into shape going to work. The airport's six miles from town."

Superintendent of Stations Thomas Needham (without hat) finished training his first group of station managers on February 1, 1948. From left are Kenneth Sersland, Eau Claire; Francis O'Keefe, Stevens Point; Charles Cox, Hibbing/Chisholm; Kenneth Schuck, Wausau; Laurence Marini, Racine; Jack Anderson, Milwaukee; Needham; Clarence Liske, Chicago; Francis Seitz, Oshkosh; Robert Allison, Madison; Richard Cooper, Minneapolis/St. Paul; William Gorenson, Rhinelander; and Ray Miller, relief manager.

The Clevelander didn't even bother to say goodbye to Needham and told Cox he was catching the next plane home. Charlie reported this sad development to the superintendent.

"It must have been the salary," he told Needham. "I couldn't have painted Hibbing in more glowing terms. By the way, Mr. Needham, I think I could do you a pretty good job as station manager."

He was promptly promoted. It was several years before Needham learned a few details about Cox's "briefing"—and by that time Charlie was not only a station manager but an institution.

Gradually, the new airline was taking shape although, as one veteran of the preoperational days reminisces, "It was more of a fetus than a healthy baby." The analogy is quite accurate, for Wisconsin Central was far from being a real airline, and its prospects looked blacker than the clouds of an approaching thunderstorm. Many employees were on the verge of quitting in the final few months before the scheduled start of service.

Even Higgins' boasts of the Electra's ten-passenger capacity proved to be empty. It was discovered that one seat had to be removed to make room for radio equipment, and Wisconsin Central's 10As by all rights should have been called 9As.

In Wisconsin Central's main base hangar at Madison, Wisconsin, a passenger seat was removed from each Lockheed 10A to make room for radio equipment.

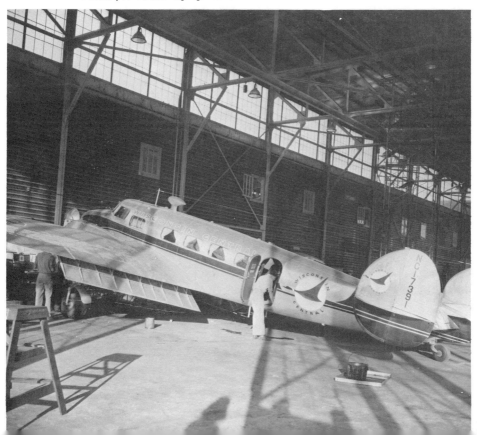

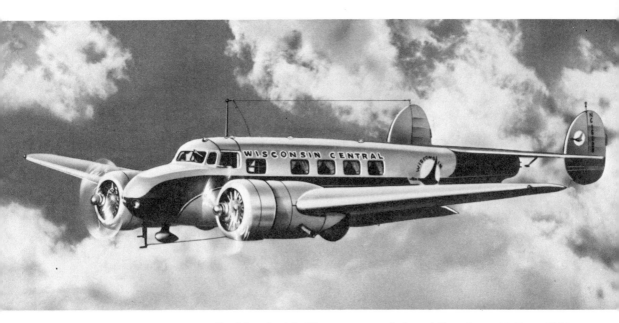

Lockheed 10A Electras served the airline from 1948 to 1951.

When the first Electra was delivered, Higgins decided it should be flown to Clintonville for a christening ceremony—"there'll be photographers there, too," he pointed out to Carr.

Carr replied that Wisconsin Central didn't have enough cash on hand to give the airplane a fresh coat of paint. Higgins came up with some money to paint just one side. The Electra flew to Clintonville and was parked as close to a hangar as the pilot could put it, the painted side exposed and the unpainted fuselage next to the hangar. Higgins was beaming proudly as photographers snapped pictures of the plane that carried the words, "Wisconsin Central Airlines," gleaming just above the cabin windows. His grin faded rapidly when he saw a couple of onlookers wander behind the aircraft, one of them shouting derisively, "Hey, the damned thing isn't painted on this side."

To identify the company's planes to the traveling public, Higgins realized the need for an official insignia. From this idea evolved a streamlined mallard duck with a circle around it. This was the first appearance of "Herman"—one of the most famous and easily recognized airline logos in aviation history.

The insignia hadn't received its nickname at that point. The origin is obscure, but "Herman" seems to have been used in cartoons drawn by a company pilot and was quickly adopted by mechanics when painting the first planes. Higgins had received a suggestion from an FWD draftsman that Wisconsin Central's symbol be a bird native to the area. The idea seemed a good one, and Karl Brocken, a Milwaukee design consultant who was doing work for FWD at the time, was asked to develop the airline's logo.

When Higgins approached Brocken, he said, "We can't afford to pay you," and added hastily, "but we'll give you some stock in the company."

Brocken wound up working another two years for Wisconsin Central before he finally got a fee—a check for $75. He spent several months on the insignia project, studying many bird designs. Higgins loved the mallard best. It was native to the North Central region and prized by sportsmen for its short flights at high speeds—very appropriate, Higgins thought, for Wisconsin Central's short-haul operation.

Brocken started with a perfect reproduction of a mallard, so detailed that the fleet would have had to be painted by a squad of Audubons. He kept simplifying the design, and from about thirty versions came the final selection—a silhouetted mallard encircled by a ring which symbolizes the sun by day and the moon by night.

President Francis Higgins (left) and Karl Brocken admire the mallard duck logo on the Lockheed 10A. Brocken, Milwaukee industrial designer, helped create the emblem in 1947.

(Through the years, there have been suggestions that Herman may have outlived his usefulness and a new image was needed. Yet in the late Fifties, an international survey called "Graphics '27" studied every airline symbol in the world for recognition effectiveness—and placed Herman second, just behind Pan American's famed globe.)

January 1948 arrived with Wisconsin Central following its familiar pattern: at least one daily major crisis, solved in makeshift and usually temporary fashion. However, the top management team had been formed—Higgins in nominal control, perfectly willing for Carr to run the airline; Pett immersed in a myriad of operating problems; and finally, burly, rock-tough Art Schwandt, the former FWD accountant who was now Secretary and Treasurer.

To support the management structure, the company was slowly accumulating a small nucleus of supervisors with previous airline experience—most of them from TWA. These included men like Bob Thorne, Manager of Tariffs and Schedules, who had worked for Carr in TWA's executive offices in Washington, and Joe Sims who left TWA and took a $50 a month cut in salary to become Superintendent of Flight Control for Wisconsin Central.

Also early in 1948, two new directors who were to have an important part in the company's future were elected to the Board at the suggestion of Loewi & Co. They were Howard A. Morey, Chairman of the Wisconsin State Aeronautics Commission, and Arthur E. A. Mueller, an industrialist from Wausau, Wisconsin.

Carr's youthful aggressiveness did not always set well with some of his older subordinates. Schwandt, in fact, got mad enough during one

At a Milwaukee reception in 1947, Hal Carr (left) and Francis Higgins unveiled a neon sign featuring the airline's logo.

Arthur E. A. Mueller, Wisconsin industrialist, became a director of the airline in 1948.

argument to punch Carr clear across his office when Carr gave him an assignment. Carr simply got off the floor and repeated the order. The incident was soon forgotten, but was indicative of the tensions existing in those early days of struggle and figurative starvation.

The airline was starting out with about a hundred underpaid and overworked employees, three heavily-mortgaged airplanes of dubious efficiency, funds so low that meeting the monthly payroll loomed as the biggest headache of all, but with one massive asset common to every man and woman who had committed his future to Wisconsin Central: determination to somehow make it go.

Thus did little Herman ready himself for takeoff into the cold northern skies—along the "Route of the Northliners"—officially designated as AM 86, "between the terminal point Chicago, intermediate points Racine/Kenosha, Milwaukee, Oshkosh, Clintonville, Wausau, Rhinelander, Duluth/Superior and the terminal point Hibbing/Chisholm; between the terminal point Milwaukee, the intermediate points Madison, Stevens Point/Wisconsin Rapids, Wausau, Eau Claire, Minneapolis/St. Paul, St. Cloud and the terminal point Hibbing/Chisholm."

"I look back on what it was like twenty-five years ago," Carr reminisces. "All I can say is that we started out with two wings and a prayer—and the Lord had to be listening to the prayer."

31

WISCONSIN CENTRAL AIRLINES

SYSTEM MAP

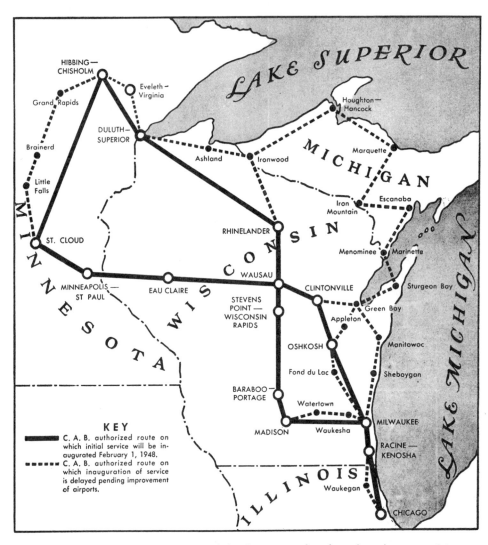

Wisconsin Central's original system showing the nineteen cities to which service was inaugurated on February 24, 1948.

CHAPTER TWO

Takeoff

It probably was inevitable that Wisconsin Central failed to meet a series of target dates for inaugurating service. Each time a deadline arrived, further postponement occurred because there were just too many unsolved problems—not the least of which was the fact that the Lockheeds weren't ready to fly yet. In January 1948, the three planes were still being overhauled, and it was a slow painful process acquiring the necessary parts and equipment.

Company headquarters in the Madison hangar resembled the birthplace of a Chinese fire drill. One day, an unidentified man walked into the corner of the building being used as the Purchasing Department. He sat down at an empty desk, picked up a phone and calmly began placing long distance calls to order airplane parts. An employee finally decided to be hospitable. "Like to welcome you to Wisconsin Central," he said.

"I'm not with Wisconsin Central," was the reply.

"Who are you with?" the employee demanded.

The answer was so vague that the police were called.

The visitor turned out to be an escapee from a nearby state mental hospital. As he was being escorted from the hangar, he looked at the collection of harried workers and fired a parting insult.

"I'm glad to get out of here," he shouted. "Everybody in this place is crazy!"

As the delays dragged on, Station Superintendent Needham had his fifteen managers performing a great variety of chores—including answering phones (which didn't ring very often) and taking reservations (which weren't requested very often). Men like Cox, Frank Seitz, Bob Allison, Ken Sersland, Ray Miller and Ken Schuck in their remote, wintery

This group gathered in January 1948 for pre-inaugural ceremonies
when Wisconsin Central announced service to Racine/Kenosha,
Wisconsin. President Francis Higgins (fifth from left) and
Executive Vice President Hal Carr (right) represented the airline.

outposts spent a lot of time in January holding bull sessions via company teletype before the welcome word finally came out: Inaugural will be Tuesday, February 24.

The historic day of February 24, 1948, turned out to be bitter cold—20 degrees below zero at most points on the system—with widespread freezing rain and snow. All flights were canceled except one, from Minneapolis/St. Paul to Hibbing/Chisholm, flown by Captain Fred Kremer and First Officer Herb Splettstoeser. The next day, many of the inaugural flights did operate. One was supposed to go to St. Cloud, but the miserable weather, plus earlier welcoming ceremonies at other airports—with picture-taking and speech-making—fouled up the schedule. With nightfall approaching, Station Manager Don Lothrop in St. Cloud phoned Needham in a panic.

"Where's the inaugural flight?" he demanded. "It's almost dark."

"I know," Needham sighed. "They won't make it into St. Cloud today. We aren't allowed to fly at night."

"For God's sake, I've got 3,000 people at the airport waiting to greet that plane," Lothrop complained. "What am I supposed to do?"

"Welcome to the airline business," Needham said softly.

Near the end of that eventful day, Higgins, Carr and Pett assembled in Schwandt's small office in the Madison hangar. It was the only warm room since Schwandt had managed to "borrow" a tiny electric heater. The four airline officials ceremoniously opened a bottle of Scotch and liberally toasted the birth of Wisconsin Central Airlines—far into the night.

The first few days and the first few months were horrendous, largely because of the worst weather in years. The Chicago-Madison inaugural flight scheduled for February 24 didn't take off for three days. When it finally left, departure was delayed until 4:45 p.m., and by the time the plane reached Milwaukee, the no-night-flying rule had to be invoked so it never did get to Madison. Another inaugural flight operated by Captain Art Hinke was stranded the first day and couldn't land in Hibbing until February 25, only to be grounded for three more days by a blizzard.

The inaugural flight from Chicago to Minneapolis/St. Paul with Captain Ralph Parkinson at the controls was operating about four hours late. When it arrived at Eau Claire, a small reception committee was on hand, including Station Manager Ken Sersland, the Mayor, Postmaster, Chamber of Commerce officials and other local dignitaries. Upon

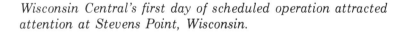

Wisconsin Central's first day of scheduled operation attracted attention at Stevens Point, Wisconsin.

completion of the welcoming program, the flight which was not carrying a single passenger was dispatched for the final leg of the trip.

As the plane was being run-up for takeoff, everything appeared normal, with all of the reception committee and bystanders observing the operation. However, when the aircraft got some 1,500 feet down the runway, suddenly the left engine failed. Captain Parkinson aborted the takeoff, and within seconds the left engine restarted.

Parkinson returned to the end of the runway and prepared once more to get airborne. Alas, this effort was a repeat performance of the first with the left engine again failing. Parkinson, however, was determined to get to Minneapolis/St. Paul, and his persistence paid off.

On the third takeoff attempt, he was a bit more fortunate. After using over half of the runway, the 10A lifted to a height of about fifty feet before the left engine failed. Parkinson had passed the point of no return, and he continued the takeoff on one engine. Then, just as before, the left engine came to life when the plane cleared the end of the runway. To Parkinson's tremendous relief, as well as his audience on the ground, the engine problem was solved, and the flight proceeded to the Twin Cities.

President Francis Higgins (on platform) and others attend a pre-inaugural ceremony at Eau Claire, Wisconsin, in January 1948. In uniforms, at right, are pilots Bill Banks and Lloyd Franke, with Station Manager Ken Sersland. (Under nose of airplane, left, is Milo Snyder, a Director of Wisconsin Central, and to his right, Mayor Orville Christianson of Eau Claire.)

In February 1948, Wisconsin Central President Francis Higgins (left) participates in inaugural ceremonies at Madison with Michael Hinn, radio reporter, and City Council Chairman William Sachtjen.

The operational report for the winter months of that first year showed only 63 percent of the scheduled mileage being flown, less than 40 percent of the flights on time, and 43 percent of scheduled flights canceled.

The pioneers tried hard—from Higgins and Carr right through the ranks. Improvising was a way of life. Cooperation was not only welcomed but mandatory, or Wisconsin Central would have folded. It was routine at Madison for mechanics to rout pilots and dispatchers out of their barracks bunks at night to help move airplanes from the hangar—because there was no money to buy even a used tractor. Two of the first dispatchers, Myron Broten and Hal Picquet, found themselves assigned to a task far removed from dispatching aircraft: they were sent around the system installing wind instruments on top of terminal buildings. Picquet drew an installation job at Hibbing.

"Worse than the South Pole," he recalls grimly. "The day I climbed to the top of the building, it was at least 25 below."

Bob Gren, a pioneer mechanic who was destined to be Vice President of Maintenance and Engineering, can never forget how cold the hangars were—particularly at Hibbing, the only Wisconsin Central maintenance base besides Madison.

"It actually seemed colder inside the hangar than outside," he says. "Every morning we'd find plugs frozen. We'd take them out, thaw them in the station manager's office, and put them back. The 10A was murder to

37

maintain because we didn't have enough spare parts. Our biggest break came when someone stumbled on a tin shed housing some old parts from a Lockheed 12—a little smaller plane than the 10A. A lot of the parts were interchangeable, and they were a godsend."

The spare parts dilemma hounded the airline for as long as the Electras were operated. Wisconsin Central's first 10A was delivered with only one spare engine and a single spare prop. Higgins bought a few surplus seats and cabin insulating material from United Air Lines for a pittance. When the airline moved from Clintonville to Madison, the entire parts stockroom was transferred in a single airplane and one automobile. The mechanics improvised and built many parts themselves. What they couldn't create was purchased from some unusual non-aeronautical sources—FWD made engine cowls, and a Madison welding company built seats.

It was a real blessing when Carr bought a beat-up, virtually unflyable Electra from the War Assets Administration for a modest $1,300 to be used as a source of spare parts.

Runway snow removal was supposed to be the responsibility of local authorities, but city streets got priority, and the airport came last. Station managers, agents, mechanics, dispatchers and pilots operated makeshift

Station Manager Charlie Cox (center) sends a teletype message in 1948 at the Hibbing/Chisholm station, which was also a maintenance base. Checking over paperwork are Mechanics Oscar Malotky (left) and Cyril Mehling.

Captain A. M. (Bill) Banks completes a 1948 training session in Wisconsin Central's Link trainer.

plows—one was a log chained to the rear end of a jeep. An approved requisition was rarer than a first edition of Shakespeare. Station Manager Dick Cooper in Minneapolis wanted to spend $7.95 for a small metal ladder—not exactly a luxury item—because mechanics were getting tired of climbing out on the wings to get to the engines. He had to go all the way up to Treasurer Schwandt for grudging approval.

Frank Seitz, hired as station manager in Oshkosh, describes the airline in those days as "just a big family—and it had to be or we would have gone under.

"About everything we did was an official no-no," he adds, "but that was the only way to get anything accomplished."

Typical was a stunt Cooper pulled when pilots complained about a huge cottonwood at the end of a runway. The tree was on land owned by a railroad employee, and he wasn't about to accede to any airline request. One night Cooper borrowed a chain saw and a car. He sawed the tree halfway through, attached some heavy ropes to the rear bumper, and eliminated one hazard to aviation.

Even passengers got into the act. A manifold once dropped from an engine at Hibbing. Charlie Cox got a 6'4" passenger to hold the manifold in place while Cox and a mechanic screwed on the bolts—Cooper having spent what was apparently the last $7.95 Wisconsin Central had available for ladders.

Captain A. M. (Bill) Banks had just touched down at the Milwaukee airport late one evening when he felt a discreet tap on his shoulder. He turned around to confront his only passenger, a rather shy, diffident middle-aged man.

"Pardon me, Captain, I hate to bother you, sir, but the cabin door is missing."

Banks frowned in disbelief. "You mean the door came open?"

"No, sir, Captain. I'm sorry, sir, but I mean the damn thing fell off."

After parking the aircraft, Banks, his copilot and the passenger then walked back to the end of the runway with flashlights and luckily found the door. They wired it on the plane and continued the trip to Chicago.

Banks' report on the incident didn't surprise Carr in the slightest. He had just had his own exposure to the somewhat dilapidated state of Wisconsin Central's equipment. The Executive Vice President was accompanying a CAA inspector through the Madison maintenance shop when the inspector noticed a loose wire hanging from a 10A. He pulled on the wire—and kept pulling until he had yanked several yards of electrical

Wisconsin Central executives enjoy a dinner meeting. From left are Director Donald Olen, President Francis Higgins, Executive Vice President Hal Carr, and Director G. F. (Joe) DeCoursin.

wiring from the aircraft. He looked at Carr, shook his head sadly, and said simply, "Jesus, what next?"

Quite early in the game, Wisconsin Central was dubbed "Whiskey Central" by everyone from passengers to other airline employees. Even the control towers used the sobriquet—and usually not in any complimentary tone.

"In reality," Carr adds ruefully, "the name 'Whiskey Central' also referred to the social habits of most of our employees."

Carr himself couldn't blame anyone for drinking in those days. There were times when not staying sober was the only way to keep from going crazy. Plus the fact that letting down a man like Francis Higgins was the equivalent of renouncing one's American citizenship. Through all the adversity, penny-pinching, mounting debts, third and fourth-hand equipment (such as the lone Wisconsin Central truck at Chicago Midway Airport, with doors attached by ropes) and general inexperience, Higgins' enthusiasm gleamed like an airport beacon in thick fog.

Although he may not have been the industry's most efficient airline administrator, Higgins, by all measurements, ranked at the top in courage. Ever the promoter, he would leap at the slightest chance to get the company a little publicity. Once, a department store staging a fashion show suggested to Higgins that he might like to pose a Wisconsin Central stewardess and a model next to one of his planes—the photograph to be used in an advertisement announcing the show.

"Great idea," chortled Higgins—neglecting to mention that Wisconsin Central didn't have any stewardesses. He merely had a secretary don a hastily-contrived "uniform" and sent her out to the airport for picture-taking.

He was constantly juggling, scheming, exuding outward confidence when his guts were being torn with worry. He once had to borrow $50,000 from the Dairyman's State Bank in Clintonville in order to meet a payroll—putting up as collateral Wisconsin Central's next expected government mail pay. Few, outside of men like Carr and Schwandt, knew how precarious the company's finances were, yet Higgins invariably put on a brave front, giving the impression he headed a carrier as successful and well-heeled as United.

On one occasion, he and Schwandt had to go to New York to try for another bank loan. Weather grounded all flights east of Chicago, and the two boarded a Pennsylvania Railroad train—paying for the tickets with the last $50 they had on them. In the club car, Higgins began ordering drinks for everyone in sight, and when the check was presented, he said expansively, "I'll sign for it."

"There's no credit on this railroad," the steward told him sternly.

"I'm President of Wisconsin Central Airlines," Higgins protested.

"I don't care if you're the President of the Pennsylvania Railroad," the steward snapped.

Back in Madison, Carr received the S.O.S.

"Send $100 care Pennsy, Pittsburgh. Urgent. Higgins."

Carr shook his head, wondering what trouble Higgins had dunked himself in, and wired the money.

There was a deep, unusually strong relationship between the President of Wisconsin Central and his young assistant. Years later, Higgins was asked if Carr's youth didn't bother him.

"Hell," Higgins replied, "I didn't know anything about running an airline, and he did—or everyone said he did. It turned out they were right, and no two men," Higgins added, "ever worked closer together than Hal Carr and I did in those frantic months when we were trying to get the airline started."

Milwaukee Station Manager Jack Anderson (right) greets Wisconsin Governor Oscar Rennebohm and the 1948 "Alice in Dairyland."

Unfortunately, the conflict between Pett and Carr continued to simmer and was a king-sized thorn in Higgins' friendly hide. The situation reached a climax when Pett erected a military-type gate across the hall leading to his department with a large sign saying *"Authorized Operations Personnel Only."* The move was obviously designed to deny the Executive Vice President admittance to the operations area.

A few days later, Higgins and Carr met with the Executive Committee of the Board to review the company's critical problems in flight operations and maintenance. After agonizing consideration, the Committee decided, for the good of the airline, Pett had to go. They directed Higgins to notify Pett that his services as Vice President-Operations were to be terminated no later than April 5.

Although he fully realized the necessity for the action, Higgins couldn't get himself to do more than drop a few hints to Pett that he was *persona non grata.* So the situation continued to be murky.

A short time later, Pett attended a stockholders' meeting of the airline over which Higgins was presiding. After routine business was finished, Pett rose in the back of the room.

"I'd like to ask the President something," he said. "Am I fired?"

Higgins flushed and just looked at Pett. The Vice President-Operations stared back defiantly. Carr, who was sitting next to Higgins at the head table, nudged him.

"All you have to say is, yes," he whispered.

Higgins gulped and finally, with a confidence he did not feel, thundered, "Yes".

Exit, Colonel Pett.

Later that evening, one of the directors contemplating the events of the meeting sagely observed, "It was a good thing Hal Carr did the prompting, or Higgins and Pett might still be standing there staring at each other."

To replace Pett, Carr wanted someone with extensive operations experience. He contacted D. G. (Del) Hendrickson, who had previously been a pilot and operations specialist with TWA, Pacific Northern Airlines, Empire Airlines and the CAA. Hendrickson was an airline veteran of the early airmail days when as he liked to say, "pilots navigated by cigars—one cigar to Cleveland, two cigars to Chicago." In April, Hendrickson was hired as Wisconsin Central's new Operations Manager.

In those days, Higgins and Carr lived in Madison's Park Hotel and frequently planned the next day's operations in the hotel bar. One night, after a lot of planning and even more drinking, Higgins suggested they take

D. G. Hendrickson became Wisconsin Central's Operations Manager in 1948.

a ride. Into his black sedan they piled, with Higgins' pet dalmatian "Speck" in the back seat.

Higgins was doing more talking than driving, and the speedometer crept considerably above posted speed limits. A siren wailed behind them.

"Oh-oh," Carr warned. "When that cop smells the liquor on your breath, you're dead. They won't let you drive a kiddy-car for six months."

"He won't smell any liquor," Higgins assured him.

"The hell he won't. He could smell it through a gas mask."

"Relax," Higgins said, "I just won't open my mouth."

They pulled over, and Higgins rolled down the window as the policeman walked up.

"You were driving pretty fast," he commented. "Let me see your license and registration, please."

Higgins, staring straight ahead, made a few gestures in the closest imitation of deaf and dumb sign language he could achieve. The officer stared.

"Is he really deaf and dumb?" he asked.

"Very," Carr muttered.

"Well, I'll be damned," the policeman sympathized. "First time I ever stopped a deaf mute. Can you talk to him?"

"Fluently," Carr allowed.

44

"Well, tell him to drive slower and be careful. I'll let him go this time. Poor guy—deaf and dumb, eh?"

"Dumb—like a fox," Carr said under his breath.

Higgins loved to regard his dalmatian as Wisconsin Central's unofficial mascot, but if a vote had been taken among the airline's employees, they would have preferred a hyena. Higgins took the dog with him everyplace, either on airplanes or in his car, and while Speck undoubtedly had many virtues, being consistently housebroken was not among them. Speck was not overly fond of flying and took out his resentment in such a fashion that the first priority of aircraft cleaning was to remove the residue of "resentment" and air out the plane.

The President's automobile wasn't much better, for on visits to Wisconsin Central stations, Higgins would leave Speck in the car while he went off to meetings and would tell an agent or station manager to let the

Francis Higgins introduces Speck, his dalmatian, to Wisconsin Central's mallard duck, Herman.

These three young ladies made up Wisconsin Central's entire reservations and teletype department during the early days of operation. They are (from left) Nancy Grab, Ruth Geist, and Pearl Schroeder.

dog out at regular intervals. The order was more easily given than obeyed because Speck was a one-man dog who snarled if anyone came within fifty feet of the car.

Bob Baker, when he was a station manager, rebelled.

"Higgins told me to let the dog out every hour," he says. "I tried it, and all I could see was teeth. I told Higgins if my job depended on walking that damned dog, he could have it."

A mechanic once charged into Higgins' office with a complaint unparalleled in the annals of labor-management relations. Speck had gone to the bathroom on his tool box.

"Just take it out, get it dry-cleaned, and I'll pay the bill," Higgins said grandly.

The station managers had their own little fraternity, formed in a spirit of mutual adversity, a common sense of humor and enough varied duties to keep an octopus busy. Wisconsin Central had no sales representatives at any of the intermediate stations. This was the responsibility of the manager, who also had to distribute timetables, load and unload aircraft, handle ground-air communications and take weather observations.

For one of the first station managers, the job was too much. He hit the bottle shortly before Captain Bill Banks was to bring in a morning flight, and decided Banks' pending arrival simply meant too much work. After landing, Banks called Needham.

"There's a little difficulty here," he informed the Superintendent.

"What's your problem?" Needham asked.

46

"It's your problem, not mine. The station manager gave me a weather report of zero-zero in fog and rain. Believe me, Tom, there isn't a cloud in the sky."

Needham had to fly up that day and fire the station manager.

Charlie Cox presented Needham with a somewhat different situation than the over-imbibing employee. Virtually all the station managers were characters, but compared to Cox they were models of convention and decorum. To Charlie, Hibbing was headquarters for Cox Enterprises, and the rest of the airline was merely a subsidiary.

No one, including Higgins, Carr, Needham or anyone else, could get him to stop trying to make a few extra bucks—for Cox, not Wisconsin Central. He once loaded his car with rabbit fur and went around the system palming it off on fellow station managers as dyed mink. He sold one station manager a jar of hair tonic which turned out to be rust remover. He peddled Irish sweepstakes tickets, fishbait, fishing lures and wild rice—the latter obtained from the Indians at a very modest price and resold by Cox at a nice profit.

Cox's extracurricular activities reached such proportions that Bob Baker, newly appointed Regional Superintendent of Stations, flew to Hibbing/Chisholm to lay down the law—no more lures or rice. He came back to Madison, his suitcase full of lures and wild rice samples.

Madison Station Agent Robert Baker assists a passenger arriving on a Lockheed 10A in 1948.

"I'm the new southern distributor," the crestfallen Baker explained to Needham. "God, Tom, he tried to sell me one of his runways, and if I could have gotten it in my briefcase, I would have bought it."

"I'll handle Mr. Cox myself," Needham said firmly.

The Superintendent of Stations also flew to Hibbing and returned later that same day.

"How'd you do?" Baker asked.

"I'm the new national distributor," Needham confessed.

Along with their other duties, the station managers were told to push flight insurance and fill out the forms for passengers because Wisconsin Central was getting a commission on every policy sold. Cox covered the wall in back of his ticket counter with dramatic photographs of crashed aircraft and led all other stations in the sale of trip insurance—"They were buying policies before they'd buy their tickets," he chuckled.

Hibbing, however, soon slumped in insurance sales. Unhappily for Cox, Needham arrived on an unannounced inspection visit, took one look at the photographic display, and roared at Cox: "Get those damn pictures off that wall!"

Whereas many station managers were a little bit in awe of the lordly captains, to Cox they were just fellow employees. He was fond of asking a

Wisconsin Central Superintendent of Stations Tom Needham (left) and Superintendent of Communications Stan Pryga in 1948.

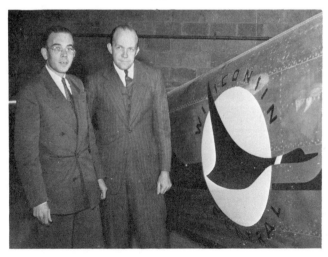

pilot, after a bad landing, "What time were you on the ground—the first or second bounce?" Only two captains ever gave him a bad time. One was Banks, who was told that Cox was planning to write a book—a no-holds-barred, this-is-the-way-it-was volume that would include a few choice anecdotes concerning Captain Bill Banks. On his next flight into Hibbing, Banks waited until he saw Cox coming up toward the rear of the plane. He suddenly gunned the engines and blew Charlie against a fence, pelting him with gravel before he shut off the power and opened the cockpit window.

"Put that in your book!" he yelled at Cox.

The other pilot who managed to instill temporary silence in the redoubtable Cox was a short-tempered captain named Bob Swennes, whose boiling point was only slightly higher than the winter weather in Hibbing. Cox made the mistake of giving Swennes an overly optimistic runway snow-depth report—telling him to expect, "a few inches." The depth was actually closer to fourteen inches, and Swennes' landing roll lasted only about twenty-five feet before the Electra just bogged down.

Cox opened the cabin door, and two big hands reached out, grabbing him by the collar and lifting him completely off the ground. It was Captain Swennes.

"The next time you let me land in this weather, I'll turn your head into a corkscrew!" Swennes snarled.

On another occasion, after landing at Hibbing/Chisholm, the Captain and a new First Officer deplaned and were heading for the station. As they walked away, the First Officer, who was not acquainted with Cox or his peculiarities, surveyed the somewhat disreputable-appearing station manager and commanded, "Hey, boy, keep an eye on this airplane till we get back."

"Yes, sir," Cox replied politely, and with that he removed his glass eye and placed it carefully on the leading edge of the wing. The First Officer watched in shocked disbelief, then stumbled toward the station muttering to himself.

With all of his idiosyncrasies, Cox was as resourceful a manager as Wisconsin Central employed. During one particularly heavy snowstorm at Hibbing, the runway markers were completely obscured. Cox gathered a pile of discarded Christmas trees and spaced them along the runway as temporary markers so flights could land and take off.

Cast in the same pioneering mold were Wisconsin Central's first pilots. If the station managers had their own fraternity, the air crews were honorary members. They worked together in cutting corners, severing red tape and ignoring conditions that would have crippled a self-respecting airline.

Dr. Ralph Bunche, Director of the United Nations Trusteeship Division, boards a Wisconsin Central Lockheed 10A in Madison.

In the spring of 1948, a group of pilots from Northern Minnesota gathered to distribute handbills from airplanes to promote the "Ice Cycles", a skating show in Hibbing. Wisconsin Central employees are (fifth, sixth, seventh from left) Agents Matt Ruper and Eddie Zeidler, and Station Manager Charlie Cox.

For example, the CAA had forbidden Wisconsin Central to land with less than a 1,000-foot ceiling and three miles visibility. In fact, "Whiskey Central" was so lowly regarded that the Weather Bureau in Minneapolis issued orders to tell Wisconsin Central pilots that fields were below minimums even when ceilings were marginal. The order was obeyed at the larger airports, but station managers at the smaller fields formulated their own rules.

"Ceiling indefinite" was a common advisory. Freely translated, it meant "it's lousy down here, but we think you can get in."

Or, "ceiling ragged," which always brought a pilot query of, "how ragged?" The response would be, "ragged."

Or, "ragged, ragged."

Or maybe, "ragged-ragged-ragged."

For every "ragged," the captain knew he'd better deduct another hundred feet from the allowable 1,000-foot limit. Three "raggeds" meant a ceiling of only 700 feet.

"They were wonderful guys," one station manager recalls fondly. "I can still see them coming in with their heads sticking out of the side cockpit windows, snow blowing all over the place, trying to find the damned terminal building. And they'd always help us unload the baggage and cargo."

The first nineteen pilots worked on the ground when they weren't flying trips. They helped the mechanics, built makeshift towbars, sewed upholstery, painted seatbelt signs, and even plowed runways.

The pilots started out, however, with a violent argument: seniority. Fifteen of them were hired on the same day—January 5, 1948—and they almost came to blows trying to agree on the seniority list. Some held out for age, others wanted seniority according to alphabetical listing, and a third group insisted on hour of hire. The controversy finally was amiably settled by simply drawing numbers out of a hat.

That first winter was as hard on the air crews as on ground personnel. "Long johns" were mandatory in the unheated cockpits. The pilots carried putty knives to scrape off cockpit windshield ice, and one captain, Earl Barron, always boarded with a small propane torch.

Nobody really loved the 10A; they merely tolerated it.

"It was the finest low-visibility approach airplane ever built," Ralph Parkinson believes, "but that's about all you could say for it. Its single-engine climb-out speed was eight feet a minute, with a maximum ceiling of only 4,300 feet. Yet I have to admit it could haul a pretty good load of ice."

The 10A had a number of annoying characteristics, such as the electrically-operated landing gear that had a habit of blowing fuses. This necessitated raising or lowering the gear with a hand crank, which in turn led to a certain incident involving the truculent Captain Swennes. He was wearing a brand-new topcoat on one flight and kept it on in the cockpit to ward off the biting cold. A gear fuse blew during final approach, and Copilot Don Planck started to crank down the gear without noticing that Swennes' topcoat was caught in the mechanism. He kept cranking until he had pulled Swennes almost out of his seat. When they finally landed, the passengers were startled to hear Planck's frantic cries of "Don't hit me! Don't hit me!"

The Electra also had aviation's only unusable lavatory because if it was occupied, the aircraft became tail-heavy. Consequently, the "blue room" was placarded on the outside of the door, *"Not to be occupied in flight"* and a second sign hanging on the inside warned, *"Not to be occupied on the ground."* This design deficiency at least had the virtue of keeping the pilots in their seats at all times and occasionally placed a passenger in a unique quandry.

Miraculously, the crews compiled a perfect safety record despite conditions that could have been classed as combat missions. Admittedly, some of it was pure luck. Captain Fred Kremer landed in Minneapolis/St. Paul on glare ice and started to skid out of control. The Electra actually went into a 90-degree slide off the runway and came to a stop directly in front of the terminal. From touchdown to final stop took less than ten seconds. One passenger aboard the plane was Croil Hunter, then President

Captain Bob Ceronsky receives directions from a Link trainer instructor.

of Northwest Airlines. He approached the pilots after everyone was off and shook Kremer's hand.

"Boy," he said admiringly, "you guys really know how to save time getting to the terminal."

One of the captains, Art Hinke, was always the essence of calmness in the most dire of emergencies. On one flight, he was letting Copilot Matt Ruper make the landing.

"Matt," Hinke said quietly, puffing on an old pipe, "we're gonna be a little short. Better add power." Ruper added power a bit late, and the wheels hit a snowbank short of the runway. Hinke didn't say a word until they taxied out for the next takeoff. He stopped the plane at the end of the runway and looked at the obvious marks left by the wheels as they plowed through the snowbank.

"Okay, Ruper," Hinke ordered. "Get out and fill those tracks with snow so they won't think I made that lousy landing." After Ruper did the job, Hinke said, "I'm willing to bet that's the last time you ever land short." According to Ruper, it sure was.

Snow, snow and more snow during those first few months. Captain Lloyd Franke got marooned in Hibbing for nine days in a blizzard and kept sending teletype messages to Madison asking for meal money. The response was deadening silence. Franke got desperate and finally sent the only message that could have brought action.

"Send money, or we sell the airplane."

Occasionally, the pilots resorted to practical jokes just to keep from getting bored if the weather happened to be good. Banks was a prime offender, and Hinke was one of his favorite targets. The only time Hinke was ever known to panic was when Banks kept talking into his mike, his mouth moving but no sound coming out. As soon as they landed, Hinke ran to an ear doctor to get his hearing checked.

Banks used to conspire with a happy-go-lucky first officer named Bob Murphy. One day Banks bought a pair of thick glasses from an optometrist and picked up a hearing aid for Murphy. The pair donned their health equipment and walked through the Chicago Midway terminal in uniform, Banks clinging to Murphy's arm and pleading, "Don't leave me. Please don't leave me."

"What? What? I can't hear you," Murphy yelled back, as passengers gaped.

Don Planck complained to Captain Parkinson once that his radio was acting up. They were both in Milwaukee where no Wisconsin Central mechanic was available, so Parky offered to fix it.

"You know radios?" Planck asked suspiciously.

"Like Marconi," Parkinson assured him.

He disassembled the radio until the cockpit was strewn with several hundred parts. Then he rose and brushed himself off.

"Sorry, Don," he apologized, "but my own flight's due to leave."

He walked off the plane, Planck shouting after him in vain to "get this damned thing back together, you sonofabitch!"

A malfunctioning radio also figured in one of the rare times that the redoubtable Captain Swennes was put down—and by a girl.

She was operating the radio at one of the smaller stations when Swennes called in to complain of transmission difficulties.

"I can't hear you," he said sourly.

"It looks okay here," she informed him.

"Well," Swennes grumbled, "you're just not putting out."

"I am too!" she said indignantly, "and I've got two guys here to prove it."

The horseplay was to be forgiven and forgotten in light of what the pilots accomplished. At Midway Airport in Chicago, Wisconsin Central crews set a record by not missing a single instrument approach for a full year, and this with nothing but ADF (Automatic Direction Finder) equipment on their aircraft. Captain Franke once made 196 landings in a single month and sixteen instrument approaches in one day (this was after the Electras got better instrumentation).

The pilots on a few occasions had to take matters into their own hands. Parkinson objected strenuously to a towering tree located on the edge of the

Green Bay welcomes the first Wisconsin Central Lockheed 10A, marking the inauguration of service in October 1948. The small white building in the background is the terminal.

runway at Stevens Point. One day he deliberately flew so low on final approach that the left main gear hit the upper branches and took off about twenty pounds of foliage. The next day, he escorted the airport manager out to the scene and pointed to the damage.

"Some plane must have hit it," he solemnly informed the manager. "Better get it down before you're sued."

The tree was cut down that afternoon.

Of the first nineteen pilots, two were fired in the first few months of operation. Banks, Ceronsky, John Downing, Franke, Hinke who is Manager of Flight Operations, Chuck Nason, Parkinson, Planck and a considerably mellowed Swennes are still flying as captains. Milt Ellyson is Manager of Airport Requirements, and Petit is an instructor in Flight Training. The others have retired or have passed away. One of the latter was Herb Splettstoeser, and there are a few stories told about this veteran.

Splettstoeser was a quiet, cautious type and had one fetish known throughout Wisconsin Central. He never took off without a full load of fuel, no matter how short the next flight. When "Spletts" died, Art Hinke was one of the many pilots attending the funeral. Hinke watched the casket being loaded into the hearse and turned to another pilot.

"I wonder if they've got a full tank in that thing," he murmured thoughtfully.

By the summer of 1948, Wisconsin Central's ragged operation began to show some progress. Del Hendrickson had introduced a number of much needed improvements in the Flight Operations and Maintenance Department, and the company's fleet had been expanded to six Lockheed 10As. Hendrickson and Carr worked well together; the airline veteran and the young executive developed a deep respect for each other's ability.

Some men who were to become prominent in the company hierarchy joined the airline around this time. One was a young accountant named Bernard (Bud) Sweet. He was a University of Wisconsin graduate working for the Veterans Administration in Madison at the time and hadn't even heard of Wisconsin Central until he was offered a job—which he took with a great deal of misgiving, enhanced by his first look at the red ink on the company's books.

In July, Wisconsin Central flew 93 percent of its scheduled miles, and 70 percent of the flights were on time. This could hardly be considered a spectacular achievement in an industry which normally completes over 98 percent of its scheduled miles. It was, however, a vast improvement over the company's earlier performance.

Bernard Sweet joined Wisconsin Central as General Accountant in 1948.

Both Hendrickson and Carr were all too aware, though, that the airline could not maintain a reliable service in the winter months to come if it were limited to a day-contact operation. Together they tried to convince the Board of Directors that the company must purchase the equipment necessary to qualify for night and instrument operation. The Board was somewhat less than enthusiastic about financing the project. At one meeting, a director objected to spending money for a VHF (very high frequency) radio system.

"I don't even know what VHF stands for," he argued.

"You don't have to," Carr retorted. "I do."

By fall, the Board gave in, and Carr won his fight to acquire navigational aids and better instrumentation for the Electras. The company bought ten H-type radio markers with its own limited funds—the CAA having refused to provide any help. By doing so, Wisconsin Central became the only airline in the country operating its own instrument airways. The ground installations alone, not including what had to be spent to modify the Electras, cost $100,000, but Wisconsin Central at last received instrument authority; day-contact flying was over.

The books showed that the company had a loss of $128,044 for 1948. A total of 11,398 passengers had been carried—fewer than what the airline now hauls every day. Their business was welcome, yet Carr was concerned that the passenger revenues accounted for only 25 percent of Wisconsin Central's income, the rest coming primarily from mail pay. He knew that passengers demanded schedule reliability, and the new instrument authority was Wisconsin Central's best hope for improving its service to the traveling public.

Higgins' report to the stockholders for the year ending December 31, 1948, noted that four of the six Electras had been modified for instrument operations, with the remaining two scheduled for conversion in about thirty days. This instrumentation had boosted the cost of each plane to $38,000—just about the total amount of cash Wisconsin Central had on hand.

Higgins ended the report with these words:

"The remarkable showing of Wisconsin Central Airlines in its first year of operation is a tribute to the pioneering spirit, loyalty and resourcefulness of the men and women in its employ."

He couldn't have phrased it better. A sizable number of Wisconsin Central's first employees had left better-paying jobs, virtually all of them because of the challenge involved in the birth of a new airline.

Thanks to men of their courage, Wisconsin Central was off the ground and climbing.

Officers and managers pose with a Lockheed 10A. From left are President Francis Higgins, Executive Vice President Hal Carr, Superintendent of Communications Gene Cleland, Purchasing Agent Stuart Lamb, General Accountant Bernard Sweet, Operations Manager Del Hendrickson, Tariffs and Schedules Manager Robert Thorne, Superintendent of Flight Control Joe Sims, Secretary-Treasurer Arthur Schwandt, and Chief Pilot Robert Ceronsky.

WISCONSIN CENTRAL AIRLINES
RADIO NAVIGATION FACILITIES

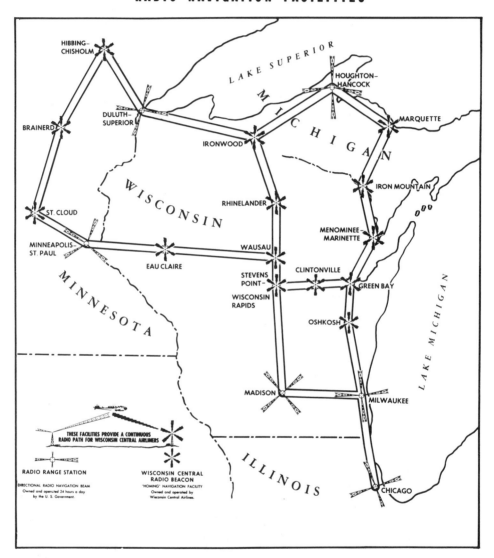

Night and instrument flying came late in 1948 with the installation of radio navigation facilities. Wisconsin Central was the only airline in the country operating its own instrument airways.

58

CHAPTER THREE

Climb

Eric Bramley is a taciturn, drawling, never-ruffled reporter who smokes a corncob pipe and is regarded as one of the best aviation writers in the industry.

He came to Madison in the fall of 1949, curiously investigating the progress of the little upstart airline that was scratching for existence. He spent several days interviewing Higgins, Carr and other Wisconsin Central officials, traveled around the system and led off a subsequent article in *American Aviation* Magazine with this observation:

> "Never let it be said that Wisconsin Central Airlines doesn't know what the word 'economy' means. A Wisconsin Central employee, in order to buy a 15-cent item, practically has to crawl in on his hands and knees and prove conclusively that the airline will shut down right now if he doesn't get it."

Bramley may have been exaggerating somewhat, but not by much. Higgins and Carr had gambled heavily—a total of more than $150,000—on the new 3,000-mile navigational aid network and 10A modification costs. For this sum, they hoped to gain at least 10 percent in schedule performance which, in turn, they figured would at least double the volume of passengers. But meanwhile, the entire operation had to be run like a Spartan army camp.

It was still the big family Frank Seitz had talked about. Charlie Cox, who with all of his reputation for wheeling, dealing and wisecracking is something of a sentimentalist, puts it in words deep in sincerity and feeling.

"This airline was built on sheer love of aviation and plain guts. No guy would have taken a job with Wisconsin Central in those days if he hadn't loved the whole crazy business even more than his own family."

Eric Bramley, Vice President of American Aviation Publications, Washington, D.C.

Bramley, one of the first objective outsiders who had been given a glimpse of Wisconsin Central's way of life, not only sensed the spirit but saw it. A veteran chronicler of airline history, familiar with the more impersonal atmosphere of the bigger carriers, he was vastly impressed by what amounted to a small-town airline.

The way the cities welcomed Wisconsin Central, for example. Bramley was surprised that some towns had chipped in to help pay for the new navigational aids. Not a great deal, it was true—community assistance saved the company about $15,000—but the spirit of cooperation was far more significant than the amount.

"Particularly," Bramley wrote, "the smaller towns feel that this is 'their' airline. They'd never had air service before, and they wanted it, as is evidenced by the $1 landing fee deal and the fact that the towns built ticket counters for the airline. Unlike many places in the U.S., these towns enjoy having Wisconsin Central planes fly over business and residential sections—it's evidence that 'their' airline is operating."

Higgins spent little on advertising; he didn't have to. He had hired, two months after Wisconsin Central began operations, a young woman named Peg Bolger to handle the airline's news bureau. If she had ever been asked to introduce the news staff, she would have stopped with herself. Actually, she didn't need much help. Any release she wrote and distributed around the system was picked up immediately and published.

Higgins himself handled public relations, his specialty and his forte. He was known throughout the area and was on a first-name basis with civic leaders and businessmen in most every community on Wisconsin Central's routes. While Carr ran the airline, Higgins was its spokesman, its chief salesman, its public image.

A regional airline couldn't have been located in a more favorable area, with many factors playing roles in Wisconsin Central's development. Train

Peg Bolger (left), the airline's News Bureau Manager, is interviewed on Madison radio station WKOW in 1949.

The mallard duck, dubbed "Herman" by employees, became a familiar sight as it flew on the Lockheeds with First Officer Tom Fowler (left), Chief Pilot Ray Ashley and other pilots.

61

Eric Bramley (left), Vice President of American Aviation Publications, visited Land O'Lakes with airline President Francis Higgins and Executive Vice President Hal Carr.

This "log cabin" (shown after the airline changed its name to North Central) is the terminal at Land O'Lakes, Wisconsin, the smallest (population 400) community in the nation with scheduled airline service.

service, to cite one, was impossible. In 1949, it took nearly twelve hours to go by train between Hibbing and the Twin Cities—a distance of only 225 miles which a Lockheed 10A covered in two hours. Minneapolis/St. Paul could be reached from Green Bay by train only by traveling due south to Milwaukee first.

The north central states are rich in industries, and the bulk of Wisconsin Central's traffic quickly became business travel. It was easier to fly than drive, and much faster than train or bus. Salesmen began covering territory in a day or two that used to take a week.

The regional airlines—at least in the formative years—expected little vacation travel because of their short-haul routes. Yet Wisconsin was a vacation mecca, and the airline found its summer traffic mushrooming. The company even started seasonal flights to Land O'Lakes, with a population of about 400, because it was in the heart of a popular resort area. Land O'Lakes became the smallest city in the United States with scheduled airline service. Its successful bid encouraged other small towns to pound on Higgins' door. Wild Rose, Wisconsin, for instance, with a population of 559 and an airport consisting of a single 1,000-foot grass runway, sent officials to Madison several times asking for airline service.

Interline business became a vital part of the traffic pattern. By the fall of 1949, about 50 percent of Wisconsin Central's passengers were flying to make connections with other airlines. It was no accident, either. Carr, thanks largely to his own background with TWA, was careful not to step on any trunkline toes, and the result was wholehearted cooperation between the big carriers and the tiny airline.

Wisconsin Central, in its second year, also hired its first sales employees. Three regional traffic managers were appointed who concentrated on the larger cities; the station managers continued to wear sales hats in the small towns.

At the time Bramley gave Wisconsin Central some rare national publicity, the airline had grown to 191 employees, each of whom received a daily report on the previous day's traffic and current financial statistics. The latter probably kept anyone from asking for a raise, but the rank and file undoubtedly appreciated being kept up-to-date.

Pilots now numbered forty, with thirty based in Madison and the rest in Minneapolis/St. Paul. The wives of the Twin Cities contingent formed a telephone club. They took turns calling various business firms, clubs and other organizations soliciting business for the airline. Bramley made a flight with Captain Lloyd Franke and First Officer Frank Musengo and commented later, "They knew more about their company than any crew members we had talked with for a long time."

Wisconsin Central's passenger service counter at Milwaukee's General Mitchell Field features a map of the airline's system and routes where service was pending.

Wisconsin Central Agent Marian McCormick serves a passenger in this 1949 photo taken at the airline's first ticket counter in the new Chicago Midway terminal building. At far right is Vern Bell, President of Bell & Farrell, Madison investment firm.

The pilots were allowed to fly a maximum of eighty-five hours a month. In June of 1949, each was averaging 84.5 hours, and Carr only half-facetiously remarked to Bramley, "I can't figure out how we missed the other thirty minutes." The Electras were getting daily utilization of nearly seven hours, flying 179,000 miles monthly—and gradually wearing out, a fact which Higgins and Carr noticed glumly.

Uppermost in their minds was the realization that the doughty little planes were too small and too expensive to maintain. Passengers were critical of the lack of room and the absence of cabin attendants. The 10A also had woefully inadequate cargo space, and Wisconsin Central knew it was forfeiting lucrative income from the area's fast-growing industrial facilities. Carr confided to Bramley that the company planned to buy at least three DC-3s in the near future, but another year would pass before the purchase actually could be made.

It was no wonder the customers complained about the cramped space in the 10A. The cabin apparently had not only been designed more for midgets than full-sized adults, but the last four seats were even narrower than the others because of the tapering fuselage. Captain Franke boarded an extremely obese woman on a flight to Eau Claire and pleaded with her to take one of the forward seats. She insisted on sitting in the rear, telling the Captain, "It's safer back here if we crash."

When they landed in Eau Claire, the inevitable occurred: she was hopelessly stuck. Franke and Station Manager Seitz had to unscrew the arm rests and almost dismantle the seat before they could get her out of the plane.

What passengers there were didn't pay much money. The highest fare on the entire system was $30.30, from Hibbing/Chisholm to Chicago. Cabin service was nonexistent, and so were any fancy amenities on the ground.

The company scrounged for additional business and never turned up its corporate nose at any type of customer—including livestock. Live ducks,

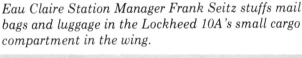

Eau Claire Station Manager Frank Seitz stuffs mail bags and luggage in the Lockheed 10A's small cargo compartment in the wing.

Wisconsin Central pilots, like Captain Bill Banks, often doubled as flight attendants in the Lockheed 10As.

Jack Dempsey, former world heavyweight champion boxer, was among the celebrities who flew with Wisconsin Central in the early days of its operation. He "fills" the small door of the Lockheed 10A.

chickens and baby chicks were common cargo items. Live frogs intended for the Chicago restaurant market were another source of income.

Wisconsin Central pilots had to double in brass as cabin attendants—the 10A was too small for the luxury of a stewardess. Not all of them liked the chore; Swennes reportedly would have preferred an engine fire. Others enjoyed the occasional contact with passengers who, in turn, welcomed the sight of a captain or first officer coming into the cabin for a brief, friendly chat. One of the latter was John (Smoke) Downing, a pilot who flew like Lindbergh and was built like Mickey Rooney.

A reporter for *Nation's Business* was on a flight with Downing and couldn't believe it when the First Officer came out to quiet a crying baby, rocking the infant in his arms while the mother readied a bottle. The newsman was further amused when he saw Downing stop by the seat of a pretty female passenger and ask if she were enjoying the flight.

"It's all right," she said with an air of boredom. "I'm used to bigger planes."

"Oh? You fly very much?"

"Quite a bit," she said hautily. "I'm a stewardess with Northwest."

Downing didn't like her supercilious tone.

"Well, I'm a stewardess for Wisconsin Central," he responded, "and you can fasten your seatbelt."

The incident with Downing and the baby nicely demonstrated how Wisconsin Central's family atmosphere extended to the passengers. First Officer Francis Van Hoof once talked a little girl out of getting airsick, and for a long time thereafter kept receiving small gifts from the child. Captain Petit deplaned from a happy flight one day and remarked wonderingly to the station manager, "On what other airline would the passengers feed *you* cookies?"

An Electra leaving St. Cloud was carrying only one passenger; the rest of the seats were jammed with express packages. The pilot had one more package to load, and was glancing around the cabin trying to find a few more inches of space when the passenger—a little old lady—held out her hands.

"Here, young man," she said, "I'll hold it on my lap."

Higgins heard about the incident and theorized, "She must have been one of our stockholders."

Express revenue was vital, inasmuch as passengers—however friendly toward the airline—were still too few. By mid-1949, Wisconsin Central was carrying more express than any other feeder line in the nation, and this

Hometown airline THAT MAKES GOOD!

Francis Higgins, the chairman of the Chamber Aviation Committee, Clintonville, Wis. (pop. 4,000), felt that the region needed an airline, enlisted the aid of Hal Carr, TWA economist, who at 27 had helped map world air routes.

Without even a small angel, the two took their project to the public, organized meetings in small towns, rang doorbells . . . sold $4 a share stock to housewives, barbers, farmers, grocers, even signed up stockholders on a Saturday night in a barroom . . . raised $620,000 capital, and started operations in February 1948 . . . made money in the third quarter of its first year!

WCA flies Lockheeds over a 1200 mile route, links up a lot of towns in Wisconsin and Minnesota with Chicago. It's short on formalities, long on friendliness . . . a superb public relations job all down the line . . . Makes money because it fills a real need! And one of the surprising discoveries WCA has made is that its small town clientele buys 20 times as many seats per M of population—as do the people in big cities!

You'll get a big kick out of following the rise of this small town airline . . . and possibly some ideas and information that may help your own business!

Look for "Grassroots Airline," by Peter Lisagor in the July issue!

Must reading . . . in next month's N. B.

Country needs "Good 5c Parking Lot,"—and Hartford, Conn. got it . . . releasing 2,100 downtown parking spaces a day . . . Lots of ideas in "How Much Do You Want Good Traffic," by Phil Gustafson.

Samba begins at 40 . . . His daughter called him "Slop-Along Cassidy" . . . middle-aged, grey, hadn't danced in 19 years . . . but he found the rumba relaxing, fox trots fun . . . See, "Look, Ma . . . !" by Jim Bishop.

Surplus and subsidy . . . The US is raising twice as much wheat as we can consume . . . farm surpluses are again major problem, need new industrial uses . . . Read "Uncle Sam's Indigestion and Dr. Brannan's Medicine," by Julius and Edith Hirsch.

Atomic automobiles . . . Radioactive-run locomotives, luxury liners, and speedboats are not around the corner . . . You'll want to read "What Can You Believe about Nuclear Fission?" by S. Burton Heath.

Eye for exports . . . Market researcher and his wife flew around the world, 32,000 miles, visited four continents, six islands . . . reports on markets . . . "Random Notes of a World Researcher," by Vergil D. Reed.

And a dozen other significant articles for business men in July Nation's Business.

N. B.—Your July issue of . . .

"Nation's Business" magazine featured the story about Wisconsin Central Airlines in their June 1949 ad previewing the July issue.

despite the limited space on the Electras. But one large cloud in the sky was the fact that growth in terms of cities served was slower than Higgins and Carr hoped.

The route development program was the primary concern of Al Wheeler, the company's general counsel in Washington. Wheeler, who had handled the original Wisconsin Central application to the Civil Aeronautics Board when he was with Roberts & McInnis, left that firm soon after the airline was certificated to become its legal counsel. William Roberts had resigned as a director in 1948, and in July 1949, Wheeler was elected to the Board. In Washington, he was energetically litigating Wisconsin Central's proposals to the CAB for routes to a number of new cities.

The company began its life by serving nineteen cities through fourteen airports. Yet the CAB had authorized an additional twenty-four cities which lacked adequate airports and could not qualify for initial service.

Through the first ten months of operation, only Baraboo/Portage, Land O'Lakes (on a seasonal basis) and Green Bay were added to the system. In 1949, total points served remained almost static for eleven months. Brainerd, Minnesota, was added, but service had to be suspended at Racine/Kenosha and Baraboo/Portage because of airport inadequacies. The latter suspension was painful to Higgins who remembered that when Wisconsin Central agreed to serve the town, he had objected to some high-

A group of Wisconsin Central employees in 1949 met Fred Myers (second from right) of the Civil Aeronautics Administration. They are (from left) Superintendent of Communications Gene Cleland; Captain Ray Ashley; Captain Duane Petit; News Bureau Manager Peg Bolger; Captain Charles Nason; Operations Manager Del Hendrickson; Myers; and Racine Manager Don Lothrop.

A. L. Wheeler, Washington attorney who handled Wisconsin Central's original application to the Civil Aeronautics Board, became Vice President and Counsel in 1949.

Mayor Levi Johnson and Jerry McAdams, Wisconsin Central secretary, (left photo) publicized the airline's first service to Brainerd in March 1949. Minnesota Queen of the Snows Joan Schellar (below) was a guest at the inaugural activities. Escorting the Queen are William Van Essen (left), Master of Ceremonies, and Joe Faust, Brainerd Civic Association Secretary.

tension wires blocking the runway approach. A few interested citizens got out shovels and dug the ditches necessary to move the wires.

On December 1, 1949, Wisconsin Central began service to upper Michigan with flights to Marquette, Hancock/Houghton, Iron Mountain and Menominee. Beloit/Janesville and Escanaba joined the system in 1950, but St. Cloud was suspended on the last day of that year, and no further points were added until 1952.

In one way, Wisconsin Central could have been forgiven for enjoying a scarcity of service inaugurals. The airline drew miserable weather for practically every one it did stage, even though the towns along its routes always turned out in force to see the first flight arrive and take off. It became axiomatic that if Wisconsin Central scheduled an inaugural somewhere, snow or rain was inevitable—and this pattern plagued the airline throughout its history.

On one of these occasions, the company was planning to start service at Brainerd on March 1, 1949. The first flight would originate in Minneapolis/St. Paul, operate through St. Cloud, and then proceed to Brainerd for the ceremonies. That day the temperature was 10 below zero, with a low ceiling and limited visibility.

Carr was waiting in the Brainerd station when he received a call from Captain Bob Ceronsky who was flying the airplane. He reviewed the weather conditions, told Carr that they had managed to make St. Cloud, but would not be able to land in Brainerd. Carr considered the situation and then said, "Bob, I've got all the city officials here, the local beauty queen, a high school band, and a big crowd. You've got to get in here, even if you have to taxi the airplane up the highway."

Ceronsky did almost that. He flew from St. Cloud at little more than treetop level and landed at Brainerd to the wild cheers of the nearly frozen spectators and the enthusiastic playing of the band.

Just as improvising, pencil-counting and scrimping became the company's way of life, so did battling the elements. The very first winter of operations was one of the worst in the history of Wisconsin, total snowfall at northern stations reaching a record 220 inches. The performance factor may have been low, but the fact that the airline compiled a perfect safety record nudged the incredible.

Wisconsin Central's safety achievements received recognition when the National Safety Council presented it with an award for completing 7,666,000 passenger miles in calendar year 1949 "without a passenger or crew fatality in scheduled passenger flight operations." The Council might have added, "How, we'll never know."

U. S. Senator Joseph McCarthy of Wisconsin was a regular traveler on the "Route of the Northliners."

There were some close shaves, like the time a Wisconsin Central plane was damaged on January 10, 1950, when a freak wind at Green Bay lifted the tail while the pilot was taxiing prior to takeoff. Prop blades, the belly and pitot tubes were bent and dented as the Electra's nose hit the ground. The 10A was out of service for nine days.

Pilot skill was an obvious factor in the no-accident record, and the flight crews, understandably, became a bit cocky. Bill Banks, however, got overconfident on one occasion. He used to set his throttles and fuel mixture in such a way that when he rolled up to the ramp, he could walk away from the plane with the props still turning. Just as some apoplectic tower operator or station manager would be screaming at him, the engines would stop of their own accord. It always worked, but Banks tried another gimmick; he would shut off one engine while taxiing in, killing the second before the plane was at the ramp. He had it timed so perfectly, the 10A's momentum carried it to precisely the right spot in front of the terminal.

One particular day, Banks had a copilot who wasn't used to these "operating techniques." Just as Banks shut down the second engine, the First Officer slammed on the brakes, and the Electra stopped 150 feet from the ramp. The red-faced Captain had to restart an engine to travel the last 150 feet. Even the cost of restarting an engine was a raised-eyebrow item in those days when things were so tough.

Some of the mail pouches carried only one airmail letter—written by a station manager so the airline would be paid for carrying the sack. The

Francis Higgins (left) accepts from Ned Dearborn, President of the National Safety Council, the first of many awards to the airline for a perfect safety record.

Attending Wisconsin Central's 1950 station managers' meeting at Madison were, standing, (from left) Arthur Schwandt, Secretary-Treasurer; Hal Carr, Executive Vice President; Bernard Sweet, Assistant Treasurer; Earl Pynch, Lyle Ferguson, John Downing, Harold Ebelt, Bob Baker, Ken Kiefer, Newt Ragan, George Tholo, Bob Allison, Ken Sersland, Frank Seitz, Dick Cooper, and Bud Green. Seated are (from left) Francis Higgins, President; Tom Needham, Superintendent of Stations; Sherry Bowen, Bob Borgerding, Charlie Cox, Chuck Vesper, Hal Schaffer, Chuck Mudron, Ken Schuck, Ray Miller, Red Behling, Roy Anderson, Larry Marini, Clyde Sundberg, Bob Smith, Clar Liske, and Bill Hicks.

*Relief Station Manager Ray Miller
transfers a sack of mail from a postal
representative while First Officer
John Hickman (left) and Captain
Walter Plew prepare to board the
Lockheed 10A.*

*Western movie star "Smiley" Burnett clowns with
Captain Bob Ceronsky (left) and First Officer
Howard Ramme in 1949.*

dependence on mail pay was a major headache. Wisconsin Central was
being paid sixty cents a mile, a temporary mail rate pending the CAB's
expected decision establishing permanent rates. It was not a particularly
generous scale, but even so, the airline's mail income for the first six
months of 1949 totaled $446,305, compared to only $100,017 in passenger
revenues.

As it did to all airlines, the Post Office Department gave the company fits
at times, suggesting its own flight schedules for better mail service. Art
Schwandt remembered their schedule pressures only too well.

"The Post Office used to figure that if you started an airplane out from
Chicago at 3 a.m., they would get faster mail deliveries and save money,"

he recalled. "They probably were right, but where in the hell could we get any passengers at 3 a.m.?"

As the tight-fisted, harassed guardian of Wisconsin Central's strained financial coffers, Schwandt was in full agreement with Higgins and Carr that passenger revenues had to be increased. For a time, he never even saw a government mail check; the bank holding the company's account insisted that the Post Office Department send the mail payments directly to the bank for deposit.

By the end of 1949, Higgins was able to report several rosy achievements to the Board of Directors and the stockholders.

—Wisconsin Central's cost per mile of operation was only eighty-two cents, ten cents lower than the average for the feeder line industry.

—The airline's loss was substantially reduced to $75,883; operating revenues had passed the $1-million mark.

—Wisconsin Central had carried 32,625 revenue passengers, almost three times the 1948 total.

—Express shipments had increased by a third, and mail had doubled.

The $150,000 spent for instrument operations was proving to be more than a wise investment. In November of 1948, Wisconsin Central completed only 46 percent of its flights, but in the same month of 1949, the performance factor soared to 93 percent. And Higgins had one more bit of potentially good news: Wisconsin Central had applied to the CAB for routes that would extend its system into Iowa and North Dakota, as well as adding new points in Minnesota, Wisconsin and Michigan—a total of over 2,500 more miles.

Wisconsin Central's 50,000th passenger, Mrs. William Corlies, Jr. of Green Bay, is honored by civic officials in ceremonies at Austin Straubel Airport in April 1950. From left are Wisconsin Central Captain Milt Ellyson, Green Bay Mayor Dominic Olejniczak and Chief of Police H. J. Bero. Mrs. Corlies, who was making her first flight, was also one of the nearly 50,000 passengers carried for the year 1950.

The company's 1950 report showed continued gains. Nearly 50,000 passengers carried for the entire year. A performance factor of 94.2 percent. A passenger load factor exceeding 46 percent—a whopping increase over the 28.2 percent of the first year and 36.8 percent in 1949. The amount of mail flown was double the previous year, and express shipments were more than double. Net profit was a healthy $92,113, with operating revenues coming close to $2 million.

The December 1949 issue of the employee newspaper, *The Northliner*, had carried a plaintive plea on the first page: "All we want for Christmas is some DC-3s." Their entreaties were about to be answered.

In October of 1950, Wisconsin Central took the plunge and bought six DC-3s costing $450,000—a quarter of the airline's total revenues for that year.

Little Herman at last was getting bigger wings.

President Francis Higgins cuts a cake in celebration of Wisconsin Central's second birthday, February 24, 1950. With him are (from left) Peg Klepetz, secretary; Del Hendrickson, Operations Manager; and Jerry McAdams, secretary.

CHAPTER FOUR

Cruise and Descent

Carr had wangled the six DC-3s at a fair price from TWA, another instance where he used his former connections to good advantage. The 21-passenger Douglas aircraft were bought for $28,000 each. After overhaul and conversion, the average cost per plane was a little over $50,000. Also purchased from TWA was about $150,000 worth of spare parts—that famine item was now a thing of the past.

The company peddled all six Electras to various customers for $35,000 apiece, raising enough money for the down payment on the TWA planes and parts. An insurance company mortgaged the DC-3s for $150,000 to complete the financing. Schwandt noted that Wisconsin Central had paid for the 10As twice over, thanks to the heavy interest they were carrying, but the little airliners had done their job.

By the time the last of the Electras made its final flight under Wisconsin Central's colors—on May 1, 1951—the six planes had flown nearly six million miles in perfect safety. Ironically, within a year after they were sold, all six were involved in crashes.

But Wisconsin Central, while it bade the Lockheed 10A a sentimental farewell, also said goodbye with a collective sigh of relief. The feelings were expressed best in a poem run in *The Northliner:*

> Blessings on you, little Herman,
> Web-foot friend with short wingspan.
> How we've waited to determine
> When and if you'd be a man.

> Long we've worried, watched and muttered,
> And our patience you'd perplex,
> As your faithful engines sputtered
> Clear from CHI to CMX.

How the big birds always jeered you.
With half-pint Herman, WIS is stuck.
And we, too, wondered—though we cheered you,
"Always a duckling, never a duck?"

But now we know our faith's well-founded,
You're fit to fly in the great air lanes.
For when we thought our hopes were grounded,
You came down with growing pains!

You've stretched and grown, your big wings sprouting,
You've twenty-one seats inside your door.
And from the rooftops, we've been shouting,
"Herman's not a 10A anymore."

So now you've got the big birds squirmin'
And we're as proud as we can be.
Blessings on you, little Herman,
Today you are—a DC-3!

The pilots were as ecstatic as anyone over the new planes, although they quickly found out that one of the DC-3's renowned vagaries was still

Wisconsin Central's first Douglas DC-3 Northliner was inaugurated into service in 1951.

present. The cockpit windshields leaked even in a light rain, and the flight crews took to wearing plastic aprons and goggles to stay dry and maintain visibility.

Nor did the DC-3 completely change the Wisconsin Central habit of improvising. One of them returned to the ramp when the captain informed the tower, "We have one more passenger than seats." A few minutes later, he radioed the tower he was ready for takeoff.

"Did you remove the passenger?" the controller asked.

"No, we put on an extra seat."

A big change that came with the DC-3s was the hiring of the first cabin attendants—all men. The new stewards had little to do, serving nothing at first, but later coffee and rolls after enough passengers complained. A well-known character among the stewards was an ex-Marine named Wade Brown, who wore his Wisconsin Central uniform with all the neatness of a sink full of dirty dishes. His idea of gracious cabin service was to stuff rolls and cups into his pockets while his hands were busy with the coffee pot. The passengers, for some reason, loved him, and he stayed with the airline for several years and even helped train the first stewardesses—who wouldn't be hired until 1954.

Economy was still the keynote. When *LIFE* magazine flew a reporter and photographer into Brainerd for a *"LIFE* visits Brainerd" feature, those words were painted on the DC-3. But to save money, the painting

Stewards came with the advent of the DC-3s in 1951. Among the first was Dick Fischer (standing). The 21-passenger aircraft had a soundproof cabin, more comfortable seating, overhead compartments, and a baggage rack in the rear of the plane.

was done hastily in watercolors. The plane encountered a thunderstorm en route to Brainerd, and by the time it landed, *"LIFE* visits Brainerd" was nowhere to be seen.

Also purchased was a Cessna 170, employed mostly for route familiarization and qualification. One day Bob Ceronsky was flying Higgins and Carr to Chicago for a meeting. As they neared Janesville, Wisconsin, Higgins suddenly clutched his chest.

"I'm having a heart attack," he groaned.

"We'd better land at Janesville," the worried Carr told Ceronsky. "Radio for an ambulance."

Ceronsky shoved the nose down in a dive that almost took the wings off. Carr patted Higgins' hand.

"Is the pain pretty bad, Francis?" he asked sympathetically.

"Yes, it's burning," Higgins muttered. "And I'm bleeding badly."

"How could you be bleeding with a heart attack?" Carr demanded. "Let me look at your chest."

He inspected the stricken President and snorted.

"Your damned cigarette lighter is leaking," he informed Higgins. "Okay, Bob, cancel the ambulance and let's go on to Chicago."

The DC-3s gave the company a chance to grow faster than anyone dreamed. With the acquisition of the bigger aircraft, Wisconsin Central found its reputation at the Civil Aeronautics Board enhanced. It not only won a five-year renewal of its franchise, but the airline was granted 900 miles of new routes. Added to the system was a route from the Twin Cities

Del Hendrickson (right), Wisconsin Central's Vice President-Operations and Maintenance, and Executive Vice President Hal Carr with the airline's Cessna 170.

Iron Mountain Manager Don Metzger (left) and Agent Gene Patrick work in North Woods surroundings of knotty cedar, the fruits of 250 off-duty hours of labor in which they gave this Michigan station a complete face-lifting.

to Fargo, North Dakota, with intermediate stops at St. Cloud, Alexandria and Fergus Falls, Minnesota.

The CAB also awarded the company a route from Minneapolis/St. Paul to Grand Forks with stops at St. Cloud, Brainerd, Bemidji and Thief River Falls. Tossed into the pot was a plum—Northwest's former nonstop authority from the Twin Cities to Duluth/Superior, as well as a seasonal route extension from Hibbing/Chisholm to International Falls (which Charlie Cox silently mourned because it took away Hibbing's title as the airline's northernmost outpost).

In a separate decision, the CAB handed Wisconsin Central a route from the Twin Cities to Chicago with five intermediate stops. All this expanded the company's system to nearly 2,300 miles and made it the third largest feeder airline in the country from the standpoint of route miles.

The franchise renewal contained a bonus—the first "skip-stop" authorization ever given a local carrier. This provision eliminated the requirement of having to make a stop at each point on every flight. The cities were protected by a requirement that Wisconsin Central had to serve them with at least two round trips a day and intermediate points could then be overflown on additional schedules. In a sense, Wisconsin Central's status as a feeder airline was changing.

Admittedly, passenger traffic was booming with revenue passenger miles soaring 97 percent during 1951. Wisconsin Central had hired, late in 1950, its first general traffic manager—big, bluff Frank Buttomer, who started

81

out with TWA and had also been in top management at Mid-Continent Airlines (now Braniff). In August of 1951, he was named Vice President-Traffic and Sales. At the same time, Del Hendrickson was promoted to Vice President-Operations and Maintenance.

Buttomer was colorful, outspoken and informal. He called Carr "Junior", and could have sold Stars of David in the middle of Cairo. He always had an eye open for promising employees, and bumped into one at St. Cloud, the young station manager. Buttomer was the only deplaning passenger off a flight and went to claim his bag. The manager, who didn't know Buttomer from Tom Mix, insisted on the Vice President's producing a claim check for the only bag unloaded!

The manager had been an Air Force control tower operator and after World War II, a steeplejack. He had taken his father to the St. Cloud airport one day and heard the agent trying to get an air traffic control clearance for a departing flight.

"Hell, I could do that job," he thought, and went to Madison that afternoon where Needham hired him as the St. Cloud station manager. The city averaged 75 passengers a month; if more than two persons boarded or deplaned a single flight, it was an occasion for rejoicing.

But Buttomer was impressed by the youngster's diligence in handling baggage, and asked Needham who he was.

On the DC-3 inaugural flight in 1951, President Francis Higgins acted as courier for mayors of cities along the route who exchanged gifts. Participating in Clintonville ceremonies were (from left) Wisconsin Central Agent Robert Gehling, Mayor Henry Laux, Higgins, Director G. F. DeCoursin and Station Manager Earl Pynch.

Participating in the Wausau Airport dedication (September 1952) were (from left) Jacob Dir; Stewardess Bonnie Emerich; Walter Roehl, Wausau Chamber of Commerce Manager; Mayor Herbert Giese; Arthur E. A. Mueller, airline Board Chairman; L. H. Hall, Chairman, Chamber Aviation Committee; Frank Buttomer, airline Vice President-Traffic and Sales; and Kenneth Willett, Vice President of Hardware Mutuals Insurance Company.

"Kid named Dave Moran," Needham replied.

"I like him," Buttomer said. "I got a hunch he'd do pretty well in sales."

Years later, Moran would succeed Buttomer as Vice President-Traffic and Sales. But right now he was a nervous, freshly-promoted rookie in a field he knew little about. Just before Buttomer transferred him into sales, Moran had a run-in with a passenger who insisted on standing in front of a fence where he was exposed to debris from taxiing aircraft. Moran finally called a policeman and had the passenger forcibly moved in back of the fence.

The next week, Moran was ordered to Milwaukee to open a sales office. His first assignment was to placate an irate passenger who had sent Wisconsin Central an angry letter complaining about rude treatment. Moran went to the customer's office. Incredibly—it was the same man he had argued with at St. Cloud.

"I'll be damned," the passenger marveled, "do you fly the airplanes, too?"

By the end of 1951, once again Higgins could present more glowing statistics. Passenger traffic had doubled to just under 100,000. Mail was up 49 percent, and express increased a fat 120 percent. But the airline's rapid expansion was costly, and net profit for the year was only $6,267. The DC-3 changeover involved heavy pilot training and requalification costs. Legal

83

expenses in connection with the route awards and certificate renewal ran high, too, and some directors—irked by the low profit yield—were making noises for even more stringent economy moves.

This led to the unhappiest development in the airline's short history—one that was not listed in the cold print of revenue passenger miles, mail ton miles, scheduled miles flown or liabilities versus assets.

For months, Hal Carr had become increasingly unhappy. He felt that Wisconsin Central had to spend money in order to prosper, and was embittered by what he considered the Board's parsimonious attitude toward any efforts to improve service. Most of the directors seemed to think that merely buying six DC-3s solved everything and assured a bright future. And on that nine-man Board, Carr could count on only two allies—Joe DeCoursin and Art Mueller.

Mueller, who had bought his first shares of Wisconsin Central stock from Carr, came on the Board of Directors in 1948. He was the lusty, outdoors-type person who loved hunting and fishing and also happened to be an astute, if impulsive, businessman. He was an investment banker and headed a conglomerate of foundry firms throughout the Midwest.

There was a strong friendship between Carr and Mueller just as there was between the youthful executive and DeCoursin. But when it came to crucial votes on key decisions, Carr—who was not a Board member—found himself outnumbered. Several of the directors were anti-Carr, others vacillated, and Higgins kept trying to compromise.

Alben W. Barkley, Vice President of the United States, was among the first to ride on Wisconsin Central's "new" DC-3s.

84

At the Board meeting on December 13, 1951, Hal Carr resigned as Executive Vice President. His resignation letter cited "general dissatisfaction with the financial policies established by the Executive Committee and the Board of Directors." DeCoursin and Mueller—and Higgins, too—tried to persuade him to stay, but by now Carr had received an attractive offer to become a member of McKinsey & Co., a prestigious New York management consulting firm.

The Board as a whole was shocked by Carr's determination to leave the company. However, the minutes of that meeting show that they "accepted his resignation with extreme regret." The Board then passed a lengthy resolution unanimously commending him for his "invaluable contribution to the development and growth of the airline." It was further resolved that this resolution "be inscribed on a plaque and presented to Hal Carr in recognition of his exemplary and meritorious service to the company."

Despite some of the directors' vehement insistence on cost reduction, the Board expressed its appreciation in a more tangible way by directing that Carr's salary be continued until March 15 of the following year.

Higgins, for one, really mourned Carr's departure; all the awesome responsibility of operating the company was now his and his alone, and he was painfully aware of his inadequacies. DeCoursin missed Carr, too. More than any other Board member, he appreciated what the young man had meant to Wisconsin Central.

"I remember what it was like before we hired him," he said. "Hell, we used to hold Board meetings in taverns, FWD offices, our own homes—anyplace that was available, and everyone was trying to run the whole show himself. It wasn't until we got Carr that we found out what running an airline was all about."

Just a few months later, at the next stockholders' meeting in April 1952, DeCoursin and Mueller had some measure of revenge. They mustered enough stockholder votes to oust several of the dissident directors and elect Carr to the Board.

The directors then named Mueller Chairman of the Board. Bud Sweet, who had joined the airline as general accountant in 1948, was made Assistant Treasurer, starting his climb up the corporate ladder.

Although Carr was now a director, he was no longer managing the company, and Wisconsin Central went into an almost immediate dive. Higgins thought the decline wasn't serious at first—just normal growing pains. He was busy trying to finance the acquisition of the additional DC-3s necessary to provide service on new routes awarded by the CAB. The financing arrangements were a veritable nightmare involving insurance companies, banks, loan companies, the issuance of additional stock and personal guarantees by some directors.

Finally, in March 1952 a minimum financing was obtained, and Higgins was authorized by the Board to buy two more DC-3s from Eastern Air Lines for $35,000 each. An additional expenditure of $70,000 was approved for the overhaul and modification of the two aircraft. While this made them somewhat more expensive than the DC-3s purchased from TWA, the price was still reasonable.

(One of these planes was to become the most widely publicized and honored DC-3 in history, aircraft number N21728. At the time Eastern sold it to Wisconsin Central, the plane already had accumulated 51,389 hours and 12 minutes of flight time since its manufacture—August 11, 1939.)

Two more DC-3s were leased from TWA, and with Wisconsin Central's expanding routes, even more were needed. Service was started to fourteen new cities in 1952, including the North Dakota points of Fargo and Grand Forks; the company now had a five-state system. But the expansion was too fast for the airline's limited resources, both in terms of equipment and personnel. Load factors on the new routes were low, and overall losses were heavy during the first four months. Wisconsin Central's sales efforts were inadequate through no fault of Buttomer who with Higgins labored valiantly, but in vain, to turn red ink into black.

In May 1952, the directors became increasingly alarmed about the condition of the company, and to provide Higgins with managerial assistance in the day-to-day operation of the airline, they hired Donald A. Duff as Executive Vice President and General Manager. Duff had an extensive background in the industry and had been President of Monarch Air Lines, one of the other feeder carriers. During the same month, Del Hendrickson, frustrated by the company's perilous financial position, resigned as Vice President-Operations and Maintenance.

In football, the sacrificial lamb when failure occurs is the head coach. In the airline business, it is the President. A disastrous first six months in 1952 and projections of further losses for the rest of the year put Francis Higgins' gallant head on the chopping block. His troubles were further swollen when Wisconsin Central suddenly was notified it would have to move out of Madison.

The Air Force, which still held title to the hangar housing the maintenance base and general office, decided it needed the facilities. Higgins' failure to change or delay that decision was another nail in his corporate coffin. In fact, the Air Force served an eviction notice for November—a grim time of the year to move the entire airline operation.

At a directors' meeting in Milwaukee on July 5, 1952, Higgins resigned as President and as a member of the Board. The resignation, however, was not to become effective until the CAB approved the equipment purchase transaction that had been negotiated between the company and the Purdue Research Foundation. (This approval was not received until October, so Higgins' position continued somewhat in limbo for several months.) The Board officially accepted Higgins' resignation contingent on the consummation of the Purdue agreement and expressed its appreciation for his valuable services to the company. They also authorized his employment as a consultant to Wisconsin Central until March 31, 1953.

The transaction with the Purdue Foundation had been arranged by Mueller and Al Wheeler in an effort to acquire additional DC-3s and to improve the airline's desperate financial condition. The contract called for Purdue to sell nine DC-3s for $90,000 each and take up the balance of Wisconsin Central's loan from an insurance company which amounted to $190,000.

The cost of these planes was considerably higher than those acquired from TWA and Eastern, but Purdue had Wisconsin Central over the proverbial barrel. The airline had to have more aircraft, and the refinancing was essential if the company was to remain solvent.

As part of the agreement, Purdue required representation on Wisconsin Central's Board—two directors, one to be on the Executive Committee and the other a Vice President of the airline. The two Board members were to be

Barbara Ann Scott, Olympic figure skating champion, boards a Wisconsin Central DC-3 in Chicago.

Grove Webster, Director of Purdue Aeronautics Corporation, served as Vice President of North Central from 1952 to 1954.

Dr. Robert B. Stewart, Vice President of Purdue University, and Grove Webster, Director of Purdue Aeronautics Corporation.

Two significant events occurred at a special stockholders' meeting in Madison on September 24, 1952. The stockholders voted to change the name of the company to North Central Airlines—to more appropriately reflect the increasing scope of the operation—and the agreement between the company and Purdue Research Foundation was approved.

This agreement provided that the Foundation would receive the company's promissory notes, not to exceed $1 million, and chattel mortgages covering aircraft and other property. Purdue was now clearly in the driver's seat.

CAB approval of the agreement came in October. That officially added Stewart to the Board, made Webster a Vice President, and removed

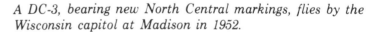

A DC-3, bearing new North Central markings, flies by the Wisconsin capitol at Madison in 1952.

Higgins as President and Director. Mueller, who had been accumulating stock and was now the company's largest shareholder, was then elected President, in addition to his position of Board Chairman.

Higgins eventually moved to St. Louis, where he set up his own public relations and research firm and did important work aiding Ozark Air Lines' expansion activities. Today, still serving as a North Central consultant, Higgins is confined to a wheelchair in his modest St. Louis home but maintains as much contact with his old airline as his infirmities permit.

In 1971, he received a long overdue honor—the Wisconsin Aviation Award—for his contribution to the development of aviation in the state. He professes no hard feelings because he had to leave the airline, but visitors can still see the flash of bittersweet nostalgia in his eyes as he recalls the early days when his faith was Wisconsin Central's biggest asset.

One of the objectives Stewart had in becoming associated with North Central was to merge the company with Lake Central Airlines. Purdue was interested in Lake Central, a small feeder airline with routes in Indiana and Ohio. At a special meeting on October 17, 1952, North Central stockholders approved a resolution providing for the purchase of 80,054 shares of Lake Central stock so that the two airlines could be consolidated. The Board then directed the officers to file the necessary application with the CAB.

For several months, Executive Vice President Duff had been struggling with arrangements for the company's move from Madison to Minneapolis/St. Paul. In October, however, the tremendous problems of the transfer were further complicated when Duff became critically ill. In an effort to keep the airline operating during Duff's absence and complete the move, the Board delegated management authority to several new committees. Besides the Executive Committee, these included an Operating Management Committee with Howard Morey as Chairman and a Development Committee with Mueller as Chairman. Virtually the entire Board of Directors was now in the act of running the airline.

On November 14, 1952, Don Duff died. At a directors' meeting the next month, Mueller resigned as President, and Howard Morey was elected President and General Manager.

Morey actually had a fine aviation background. In addition to serving as Chairman of the Wisconsin State Aeronautics Commission, he had been a pilot for years and owned the Morey Airplane Company, an aircraft sales and service organization located in Middleton, Wisconsin. He had joined the Wisconsin Central Board in 1948 and was only too well acquainted with the company's problems. Unfortunately, he lacked badly needed airline experience and came close to presiding over North Central's total collapse.

Howard Morey, Chairman of the Wisconsin State Aeronautics Commission, was President of North Central from 1953 to 1954.

Certainly, Morey inherited a can of worms. He assumed his office less than a month before the airline had to move from Madison to the Twin Cities. Limited space was found at Wold-Chamberlain Field for the maintenance base, and the general office was housed on the second floor of a building at 3300 University Avenue, S.E., Minneapolis.

North Central's Annual Report for 1952 summed up the moving difficulties in this fashion:

> "An agreement with the Minneapolis-St. Paul Metropolitan Airports Commission provides that, as soon as possible, adequate hangar and maintenance facilities will be made available. Our move, however, created a temporary problem of housing. It was necessary to separate the maintenance functions and perform daily inspection and repairs in a public hangar; and to establish aircraft overhaul, stocks and stores at a second location. This factor, together with a loss of experienced personnel who did not desire to move to the new location, caused a disruption in our maintenance program with resultant delay and cancellation of flights."

Only an annual report to stockholders could have phrased a generally "snafued" situation in such calm words. Higgins' departure was resented by many of the pioneer employees, and the shift to the Twin Cities was not exactly popular. The airline's fifth anniversary on February 24, 1953, was no cause for celebration; morale was low, and Morey's leadership

90

uncertain. Worst of all, the suddenly evident influence of the Purdue organization split the Board of Directors and the Executive Committee into warring factions.

Stewart in particular, by his rather dictatorial manner, created an abrasive situation on the Board. As one director described it, "Stewart assumed he was the professor and the Board members the students. Among other things, he would infuriate the directors by frequently interrupting meetings to take personal telephone calls while we were trying to consider matters vital to the survival of the airline."

There definitely were important things to discuss. Such as the $101,474 loss suffered during 1952. Or the proposed merger with Lake Central Airlines. The latter wasn't a bad deal. The agreement called for North Central to purchase 96 percent of Lake Central's stock at a bargain price: Lake Central's net book value after settlement of a pending mail rate case with the government, plus $10,000 cash. The book value was virtually nil, and North Central stood to take over the smaller airline for only $80,000. Routes of the two airlines dovetailed nicely, and hopefully the CAB would soon approve the merger application. (As it turned out, the CAB wouldn't act on it for another four years.)

DC-3s parked at Chicago Midway Airport in July 1953 show the airline in transition. One (at left) still bears Wisconsin Central markings, and the center plane has North Central, with "formerly Wisconsin Central" near the door. The aircraft at right features the complete red and white "feather motif" with blue lettering and insignia.

The year 1953 was one of total turmoil although one couldn't arrive at this conclusion by reading the annual report. It phrased disaster in terms of progress and accomplishment, mostly by emphasizing the positive while sugarcoating the negative.

There were, it was true, positive things to report. Detroit, Grand Rapids and Lansing, Michigan, had been added to the system—for the first time linking the Upper and Lower Peninsulas of the state with scheduled air transportation. Thief River Falls and Fergus Falls, Minnesota, with Manitowoc, Wisconsin, also joined the system. Seasonal service was begun to International Falls, Minnesota.

The DC-3s carried 217,663 revenue passengers, more than the airline had hauled in the first four years combined. The total represented a 42 percent jump over 1952. Of the fourteen local service airlines flying at the time, North Central ranked first in express and second in passengers and mail.

But 1953's net loss was $119,367, the second consecutive year in which the company had lost over $100,000, and things were getting worse instead of better. Early in 1954, operating costs zoomed to $1.25 a mile. Losses were running $58,000 to $72,000 a month. North Central's unpaid bills by the end of March totaled $511,000, and the airline was reeling.

The company was overdrawn in most of its bank accounts and finding it almost impossible to meet payrolls. Creditors were clamoring to be paid. The airline's fuel supplier and insurance underwriter were both threatening to terminate their services because of long-outstanding unpaid

Employees at Madison try out the new hydraulically-controlled airstair door on the DC-3. From left are Betty Pederson, payroll clerk; Chet Matthews, station agent; and Bernard Sweet, Assistant Treasurer.

Station managers met in 1952 with President Howard Morey (seated, second from left) and department heads. From left are (standing) Vice President-Traffic and Sales Frank Buttomer, Ken Sersland, Dick Cooper, General Traffic Manager Clar Liske, Secretary-Treasurer Art Schwandt, Ray Miller, and Don Lothrop; (seated) Ken Schuck, Morey, Frank Seitz, Superintendent of Stations Tom Needham, Larry Marini, and Bob Allison.

bills. Several of the DC-3s were impounded by cities for nonpayment of landing fees.

Credit was so shaky that on one flight Captain Parkinson bought fuel with his own gas credit card because the supplier refused to honor North Central's.

In this financial crisis, the company turned to the Civil Aeronautics Board for relief in the form of a mail pay hike, but the CAB—which had already granted several increases—flatly refused. On February 12, 1954 the Chairman of the CAB wrote a letter to Morey with copies to each director saying, in effect, that although no certificated airline had ever gone bankrupt, North Central was apparently going to have that dubious distinction.

Specifically, the CAB's letter stated:

"North Central's financial problems are of grave concern to us. The Board must emphasize that the carrier has exhausted the temporary rate device as a means of meeting its present critical financial problems and cannot expect further temporary mail pay relief for these problems. The Board, therefore, must again place the management of the company, including its Board of Directors and officers, on notice that the solution of the carrier's problems is the immediate responsibility of management."

Morey's solution was to drastically cut schedules. Aircraft utilization fell to about four hours daily; some DC-3s actually sat unused on the ground for so long that the tires rotted. Morey continued to slash schedules, eliminating any flight that wasn't at least breaking even. It was a fatal error. The simple fact was that the direct cost of operating these flights was saved, but the revenue was lost; while the indirect cost, spread over the smaller operating base, increased dramatically. The result was an even larger loss than before the schedule reduction.

In line with this retrenchment, one of the company's few route cases before the CAB was a request to abandon nearly 20 percent of the system. Efficiency and operating performance fell to a new low, and cities on North Central's routes were protesting loudly. The airline was fast losing one of its most priceless assets—passenger loyalty.

The infighting on the Board of Directors was brutal. Mueller and DeCoursin were the Young Turks, as they had been since Carr's departure as the Executive Vice President, and both admitted freely that losing Carr was a major mistake.

While North Central continued its plunge, DeCoursin went to work on Chairman Mueller.

"This airline's going under," he warned. "You know and I know who could save it. Let's quit pussy-footing around and try to get Hal Carr back."

Mueller hesitated.

"I've known Howard Morey for years," he said. "I agree with you about Carr—but will you tell Morey he's through?"

"You're damned right I will," DeCoursin snapped.

Mrs. Eleanor Roosevelt flew on a North Central DC-3 to St. Cloud, Minnesota, on October 23, 1953. Assisting her are Steward Wade Brown (in doorway) and Station Manager Harold House.

Hal N. Carr became the nation's youngest airline president when he was named head of North Central in April 1954.

During this time, Carr, as a member of the firm of McKinsey & Co., was busily engaged as a management consultant to a number of major corporations and government agencies. He had been elected to several Boards of Directors and was a Professorial Lecturer of management engineering in the Graduate School of Business Administration at American University, Washington, D.C.

Carr wasn't enthusiastic about leaving all this to get into what appeared to be a hopeless situation. However, DeCoursin and Mueller eloquently appealed to his loyalty by pleading that if he did not return, the airline he had been instrumental in starting would surely go out of existence. After several sessions with the two directors, Carr agreed to head up the company with the understanding that he would probably return to McKinsey & Co. eventually, whether or not North Central could be saved.

At a directors' meeting on March 9, 1954, the Board accepted the resignation of Howard Morey. Chairman Mueller was then authorized to engage Hal Carr as the airline's new President and General Manager. The Board also directed that the company would be managed by Vice President Grove Webster until Carr could assume his position on April 7.

Soon after that, Mueller returned to Minneapolis and called a meeting of all the airline's executives to announce the name of the new President. He milked the occasion for all the drama possible. Mueller recounted the company's precarious situation at length and in great detail. Those assembled were literally sitting on the edges of their chairs waiting for Mueller's announcement. Finally, after a long forty-five minutes, he raised the verbal curtain on Morey's successor.

"The name of the new President of North Central Airlines is"—long pause—"Hal N. Carr!"

There was a stunned silence broken finally by Buttomer's booming voice, "Hal Carr," he roared, "well if anyone can bail us out, maybe that sonofabitch can!"

There was a general feeling of relief in the group. Little Herman now had a leader—one who, at the age of 33, was the youngest president in the airline industry.

Flying into the summer of 1954, North Central started with new hope.

CHAPTER FIVE

Restart

Carr got a firsthand example of North Central's disintegrating financial state as soon as he took over. The Minneapolis hotel where he was staying requested that he pay his bill daily.

North Central had been the victim of a multitude of management. In the less than three years since Carr had left, the airline had been run by Higgins, Duff, Mueller, several committees of the Board, Morey and Webster. Small wonder that even the most dedicated employees were disheartened and in a general state of panic about the company's future.

Carr's first job was to stall the major creditors. He talked them into granting a 90-day grace period which gave him enough breathing room to start performing his miracles.

The second job was to clean house, and he used an axe, not a broom. Quite rightfully, he was greeted with nervousness, suspicion and real fear because he began chopping off executive heads like a French revolutionist in Bastille days.

Bud Sweet was promoted to Treasurer and Assistant Secretary. Carr shifted Schwandt to a new post: Vice President of Industrial Relations. To replace the Operations Manager, he hired from the CAA Alvin D. (Nemo) Niemeyer, who had spent years helping to develop the nation's airways system. The new Chief Pilot under Niemeyer was Gaile F. (Red) Wallis, a North Central captain and an ex-Marine Corps fighter pilot. To both, Carr gave a flat order: "Get those flying costs down."

They did. Niemeyer discovered that North Central's operating procedures had changed little since the days of the 10As. He revised these overnight to conform with DC-3 performance capabilities. He also came up with the idea of reducing landing minimums by using commercial radio

North Central's new management team at a meeting in 1954. From left are Bernard Sweet, Secretary-Treasurer; Arthur Schwandt, Vice President-Industrial Relations; Hal Carr, President; Frank Buttomer, Vice President-Traffic and Sales; R. H. Bendio, Director-Maintenance and Engineering; and A. D. Niemeyer, Operations Manager.

stations as letdown aids. The pilots themselves offered to cut at least one minute off each flight over each route segment, and in a single month the cost per mile for fuel dropped from 12.9 cents to 12.3.

Another money-saving trick was the rolling magneto check. Niemeyer and Wallis got the pilots to lock the aircraft tailwheel, apply the brakes lightly and then run up the engines while the plane was moving. It saved about two minutes at every stop—a minor item, unquestionably, but a lot of minor items were adding up to a 180-degree change in course.

Carr may have been welcomed with jitters by some North Central officials, but the rank and file regarded him as a savior. They showered him with suggestions, offers to help, and promises of complete cooperation. The day Carr assumed office, he asked every employee who could be spared from his job for a few minutes to gather in the maintenance hangar. He climbed on an engine stand, looked at their worried faces, and spoke briefly and bluntly.

"It's just this damned simple," he told his sober audience. "We're broke. But I think we can pull out of it if we all work together."

Knute Rockne couldn't have made a better fight talk. About 90 percent of the cost-cutting ideas came from company personnel, and no suggestion

98

was too piddling or farfetched for Carr to consider. For example, an employee proposed that the company's teletypes be set on single-spacing instead of double; this move saved a modest $90 a month. One group offered to take a pay cut, and the station managers told Carr they'd work without pay for a week. Carr refused.

"If we can't pay the going rates, we shouldn't be in business," was his answer.

The general office was in Minneapolis, overhaul maintenance in a Wold-Chamberlain Field hangar, line maintenance at another hangar, while flight control was in the terminal building. Carr moved almost the entire operation into a single hangar, immediately wiping off the books $26,000 in annual costs.

Every department got into the economy act. Maintenance saved $7,800 a month by improving techniques and operating times. Flight Operations reduced costs by $7,035 monthly through Niemeyer's new procedures, plus simplifying manuals, altering flight clearances and forms, and having the Chief Pilot fly the line thirty hours a month. The general office knocked more than $4,000 a month from costs with various administrative reforms—they were literally counting pencils. In Traffic and Sales, Carr ordered an immediate $5,000 advertising cut and instituted a service charge on passes. He arranged for Northwest Airlines to handle downtown Detroit ticketing and reservations, and fired a few traffic employees he considered surplus.

There were some personnel cuts in all departments, but Carr refused to indulge in wholesale firings. His approach was to increase the airline's service to effectively utilize the present employees, rather than drastically reduce personnel to fit a curtailed operation.

North Central moved its headquarters to this building at the Minneapolis-St. Paul International Airport in 1954. Offices were mainly on the second floor, overlooking a hangar bay where maintenance was performed.

Several people in the top echelon were fired, and some others resigned—Buttomer among them—but Carr went personally to Buttomer's office and asked him to reconsider. Buttomer shuffled nervously and indecisively through the papers on his typically cluttered desk and finally growled, "Okay, Junior, I'll stay, but I'm going to keep my bags packed in case I have to bail out."

North Central had lost nearly $200,000 in the first three months of 1954, with monthly losses from $58,000-$72,000. During April, the trend was slowed down; May and June together netted $67,000, and July showed $62,000 profit—a most dramatic about-face.

Flight schedules were improved and expanded. North Central, for example, had been operating twelve round trips between Milwaukee and Chicago, a schedule which left long turnaround times in Chicago and was money-wasting because of idle aircraft. Carr upped the schedule to twenty-two daily round trips—after ascertaining that a 31 percent load factor on the additional flights would pay for the costs of operating them. The load factor for the new flights in the first month was 47 percent and never fell below that figure.

Aircraft utilization was boosted from four hours, twenty-eight minutes daily in March to six and a half hours by August; miles flown went from 355,000 to 543,000.

No area of inefficiency or sloppiness was too small to catch Carr's eye. He dropped in on Maintenance one day and noticed that some newly-received

One of three regional meetings for station managers was held in July of 1954. The Twin Cities group included (seated from left) Vice President-Traffic and Sales Frank Buttomer, Superintendent of Stations Thomas Needham and President Hal Carr. Standing are (first row from left) Charles Cox, Frank Seitz, Chester Matthews, Senior Agent James Meyers, District Traffic and Sales Manager John Hammer, and Ray Miller. Second row (from left) James Butala, Thomas Christensen, Harold House, Robert Frank, Robert Borgerding, Paul Nygren, Edward Noga, Kenneth Schuck, Harold Ripley, and Keith Cornell.

Expanded and improved schedules in 1954 attracted new air travelers, including summer vacationers who flew to the King's Gateway Airport serving Land O'Lakes, Wisconsin.

parts looked tinny and poorly built. Joe Dick, a veteran mechanic, watched curiously as Carr turned a part over in his hands, frowning as he examined it.

"I could be wrong," he said to Joe, "but I'd be afraid to put this on a Model-T, let alone one of our airplanes."

That was all the long-suffering mechanic needed.

"Mr. Carr," he said earnestly, "about 50 percent of the stuff we're getting from suppliers is no good. We can't even use it." From then on, Maintenance paid considerably more attention to receiving inspection, and the quality of parts improved immediately.

Carr also ordered the entire fleet (now down to eighteen aircraft) repainted and cleaned—some of the DC-3s were still carrying Wisconsin Central markings.

In three short months, the airline was completely reorganized and returned to a profitable position. Scheduled miles were increased nearly 50 percent, and employee morale soared as operating efficiency and flight performance improved dramatically. One reason for this was that maintenance cancellations dropped from an industry high of twelve per 1,000 hours in 1953 to an admirable low of three in 1954.

Slashing costs and improving the operation were only two of the salvos Carr fired. Raising equity capital was another dire necessity. Before the year was up, North Central made a public sale of $215,000 in convertible debentures. Even before this money poured into the coffers, the airline was paying about three months of its long overdue bills every month, and the fresh financial transfusion allowed it to clean up all obligations.

Included among the debts paid off in full was the $1 million to Purdue—which, in turn, led to the resignations of Stewart and Webster from the Board of Directors. In more ways than one, Carr had his airline back. He swept out the Purdue influence by refinancing the loan through the Northwestern National Bank of Minneapolis—with North Central's DC-3s as collateral—at a lower interest rate than the airline had been paying. The Board itself was now down to a more cohesive and compatible seven members.

Carr still wasn't happy with the fleet appearance and had Brocken redesign the interiors with a new color scheme. Also added to the DC-3s were carry-on luggage racks, five more seats—making twenty-six (which boosted revenues with little increase in operating costs), and the most startling innovation of all—stewardesses!

None other than famed columnist Westbrook Pegler indirectly convinced Carr that North Central should have what every other airline already had—female cabin attendants. The volatile, crusty writer had taken a North Central flight, as he reported in a column, that was fine in every respect except for being greeted by a 190-pound steward instead of a pretty girl. The Pegler column reached Carr's desk shortly after he assumed the presidency, and the first stewardess class graduated in May.

Four girls were in that class: Sylvia Kish, Hammond, Indiana; Janice Kinna of Frederick, Maryland; Delores Trevison, Milwaukee; and Gloria Bishop, Canajoharie, New York. So hastily had they been hired that Carr

At a reception in 1954 promoting service to Land O'Lakes, Wisconsin, are: (back row, left to right) David Moffitt, Manager-Public Relations; A. D. Niemeyer, Operations Manager; Travel Editor, Chicago Tribune; G. F. DeCoursin, Director, and Mrs. DeCoursin; Hal Carr, President; Frank Buttomer, Vice President of Traffic and Sales; R. H. Bendio, Director of Maintenance and Engineering; A. L. Wheeler, Vice President-Counsel; Station Manager Gilbert Bromenschenkel. (Front row) Clarence Liske, Sales Manager; David Yuenger, Green Bay Press Gazette; Arthur E. A. Mueller, North Central Chairman of the Board; Robert Grover, Director; Werner Christensen, Director; and (seated) Sherm Booen, Twin Cities aviation newcaster.

Sylvia Kish, North Central's first stewardess, was hired in May 1954.

didn't have time to buy complete uniforms or establish anything more than a makeshift training course. All four had gone through a private airline school in Minneapolis, however; and Steward Wade Brown was assigned the job of completing their education. Fortunately, he stuck to the basics, without imparting some of his own unconventional theories of cabin service.

Jan Kinna Hicks (now married to a North Central captain) remembers that earliest stewardess class:

"The first day, they told us to go out and buy a blue skirt and a white blouse which would be our uniform until we got regular ones. That same day, they sent us to a men's store to be measured, and gave us a twenty-page manual to read. The second day, Brownie showed us through a DC-3 in a hangar. On the third, we all took an observation flight. The fourth day, we started flying the line. Brownie's final word of advice was to take along plenty of reading material and food."

The first stewardesses had little to do in the way of cabin service. North Central had stopped serving coffee during the Morey regime as an economy measure, and it wasn't offered again until December of 1954. Mary Ogle, who graduated in the second class, used to start out from Chicago with hot coffee in a thermos jug, and relates, "By the time we got to Milwaukee, I was serving iced coffee."

Weather was the biggest problem the girls faced—the DC-3 was either too hot or too cold. On a typical winter flight, the only thing a North Central stewardess removed in the cabin was her gloves; most of them kept their coats on. But winters were preferable to hot summer days when it was not uncommon for an entire planeload to get airsick. Joan Northern Livingston

103

Three of North Central's first four stewardesses try on their new uniforms in 1954. From left are Janice Kinna, Sylvia Kish and Gloria Bishop.

This welcoming group (below) was part of the program promoting North Central flights to International Falls, Minnesota, in 1954. North Central Vice President Frank Buttomer is third from left, with Stewardess Jan Kinna in center front.

Stewardess Sylvia Kish prepares to embark on her first flight with Captain Bill Evans and First Officer Elliot Nelson.

remembers having to close the cockpit door during one flight because the sound of heaving was getting to the pilots.

"When we reached Chicago," she adds, "they had to take every seat out of the plane for cleaning and airing."

For the first two months, the stewardesses wore anything they wanted so long as the blouse was white and the skirt blue—but Jan insists: "It was better that way because the first uniforms were pitiful. Later we had one that was even worse—every time you sat down, the skirt came loose; and when you stood up, it would fall off. It got so we couldn't take a flight without a supply of safety pins."

The stewardesses flew about eighty hours a month. They cleaned the airplanes themselves, shivered in the winter, roasted in the summer, marveled at the day North Central put a magazine on its planes for the first time (it was *Country Gentleman*), kidded the pilots, got used to changing roommates (Mary Ogle had forty in ten years and was asked by the mailman one day, "Who's the desk clerk in this hotel?"), and became part of a regional airline's way of life.

North Central pilots, being 100 percent, red-blooded American males, welcomed the influx of pulchritude as a sign that the airline was growing up. But they quickly learned what their brethren on other carriers had learned long ago: the awesome presence of four stripes doesn't keep a stewardess from occasionally putting a captain in his place. Even Bill Banks was taught a lesson.

Banks was nearing Hibbing on a DC-3 flight one winter night and received a weather report that the temperature there was 19 below zero. He thought the passengers might like this information and rang for the stewardess to come to the cockpit. The procedure for summoning a stewardess to the DC-3 flight deck was a three-bell signal. Banks, however, lost count and rang four times—the signal for an inflight emergency.

In the back of the passenger cabin, the stewardess—who happened to be fairly new with the airline—was a young lady known for maintaining a rather formal demeanor with the passengers and flight crews.

She reacted very professionally to the Captain's distress signal, managing to freeze a smile of false courage on her face, and went down the aisle urgently telling the passengers to prepare for an emergency landing.

"Will you please fasten your seat belts and extinguish all smoking material," she intoned. "Also remove all sharp objects from your pockets and, ladies, will you take off your high-heeled shoes."

"Now," she continued, "will everyone lean forward, place your head on your lap and fold your arms."

She continued to the cockpit, her heart pounding, determined to live up to the courageous airline stewardess tradition. Once there, she tapped Banks on the shoulder with a shaking hand and gasped, "What is it, Captain?"

"Temperature's 19 below in Hibbing," Banks cheerfully informed her.

The young lady glanced back at the twenty-five terrified passengers, all sitting with their arms folded over their heads, looked at Banks and acidly said, "No shit!"

On another occasion, Carr was on an early morning DC-3 flight to Madison with a brand-new stewardess whose hasty training had been on the skimpy side (a far cry from what a North Central flight attendant goes through today). After they had been flying awhile, Carr saw that the propeller on a faulty engine was being feathered, and he quietly summoned the rookie stewardess.

"The captain has feathered a prop," he said. "Maybe you should mention it to the passengers."

"Yes, sir, Mr. Carr," she beamed.

Carr watched her march down the aisle confiding to everyone aboard—in the same breathless tone she would use if she were revealing her engagement—"The captain has feathered a prop—the captain has feathered a prop—the captain has feathered a prop."

After happily delivering this message to all the passengers, the stewardess returned to Carr's seat.

"I've told everyone," she reported, proudly. "By the way, Mr. Carr, what does it mean to feather a prop?"

"It means," Carr said gently, "we've lost an engine."

With this news, she promptly fainted.

The flight attendants were under the direction of Jim Palm who had managed the stewards before the advent of the girls. In April 1955, Palm was named a district traffic manager, and the airline's first Chief Stewardess was hired. She was Kathy Leddick, a registered nurse who had been one of the original stewardesses on Northwest Airlines' Orient routes and had also flown as a hostess with American Airlines.

North Central had about 100 stewards when the girls were hired. A half-dozen went into flight training, and another twenty-five or so were shifted to various ground jobs. The remainder kept flying until they eventually left the company.

A couple of months after stewardesses began to fly the line, Carr hired another woman employee—a new executive secretary. He had a temporary one, but wanted a career girl with outstanding ability and judgment.

106

Charlotte Westberg joined North Central as secretary to President Hal Carr in August 1954.

Department heads sent him several recommendations, but Carr wasn't satisfied with any of them and finally put a blind ad in a Minneapolis newspaper to the effect that an airline president was seeking a secretary.

The company's personnel manager came into Carr's office a few days after the ad ran, waving an application folder.

"I've got the girl for you," he said.

"Is she good?"

"Based on what's in here," the manager replied, "she should be president of a corporation."

Carr opened the folder and looked at the name on the application form. It was Charlotte Westberg.

A Minneapolis native and a graduate of the University of Minnesota, Charlotte Westberg had been secretary to the President of a Los Angeles advertising agency. She had been with several public relations firms and had also worked for Chicago & Southern Airlines before its merger with Delta. While in the Twin Cities for a visit, she saw the ad and was mildly curious—enough so to write out a resume, on a borrowed typewriter, and put it in the mail.

Two days later, Charlotte was called and asked to come to the airline to take some tests. She met Carr briefly and returned home, not particularly impressed by the frantic atmosphere around North Central in those recovery days. A week later, the personnel manager phoned her again.

"Mr. Carr wants to see two applicants for final interviews," she was told, "and you're one of them."

Charlotte started out to the airport and en route decided she wasn't interested in the job or in returning to the Twin Cities, a decision which she relayed to the personnel man who greeted her.

"I only kept the appointment to advise you I'm withdrawing my application," she said.

"Don't tell me; tell Mr. Carr," the personnel interviewer pleaded. "At least see him. He was very impressed with your qualifications and is expecting you. If you leave, I'll probably be the one looking for a job!"

So she agreed to see Carr once more. After he described the airline's future in glowing terms, Charlotte accepted the position, thinking she would stay about six months while looking for something a bit less hectic in a warmer climate. Nineteen years later, she is still with North Central—having been promoted to staff assistant to the president in 1955 and named corporate assistant secretary in 1962, a post which made her one of the top women executives in the airline industry.

By the end of 1954, Charlotte knew she had figuratively married the airline. "I had a front row seat watching North Central's recovery," she recalls, "and I just couldn't leave until the job was done. Only it was never really done. The day I started to work for Mr. Carr, we had eighteen airplanes and 600 employees. In my first five years, the airline doubled in

Captain Matt Ruper (left) checks weather data with Joe Sims, Manager of Flight Control. Both men were with the company when scheduled service began in February 1948.

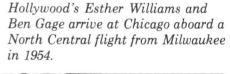

Hollywood's Esther Williams and Ben Gage arrive at Chicago aboard a North Central flight from Milwaukee in 1954.

size; and in the next five, it tripled. It wasn't easy at first. You got the feeling that if you hadn't started out back in the days of Clintonville and Madison, you were a johnny-come-lately. Now they all think I came with the Ark!"

From the beginning, she was the perfect model of an executive secretary. Carr demanded efficiency, total loyalty, an uncanny sense of what was right or wrong, an indefatigable memory, a fetish for perfection and the ability to keep one's mouth shut. Charlotte had every attribute. In turn, her respect for Carr was boundless. She got to know him as few North Central employees do and draws an interesting and revealing portrait of the man who saved the airline from extinction. To quote her:

"People are always asking me what's it like working for Mr. Carr. It's easy to answer. There's nothing to it—unless you make a mistake. He always forgives you, but heaven help you if you make the same mistake twice. His information is fantastic. I don't know where he gets it, but he knows everything that goes on around this airline. He expects loyalty, but he's loyal himself—to every man and woman in North Central. I've seen him refuse to see other airline officials or businessmen because he already had an appointment set up with an employee.

"I got used to his habits very quickly. For instance, he abhors being interrupted when he's working, and he's always working. So I try to type the messages and questions. If it's on a piece of paper, you'll get an instant answer in writing because he wants it off the desk. His memory is amazing, and his mind is like an encyclopedia. I've never heard him issue an order without prefacing it with, 'please,' and it's always in simple, concise language. He chooses competent people to run the departments, gives direction, and then lets them do their job. Carr dislikes large staff meetings, preferring to deal directly with the executive involved in any project or problem. To him, big meetings are not good management because one department head's troubles aren't necessarily another's. He is meticulous in his use of time. But more than anything else, his optimism, enthusiasm, and faith in the airline's future rubs off on everyone."

Charlotte's description of Carr as an executive is significant; he is a devout advocate of what he calls "the techniques of scientific corporate management," and it was sound management practices that propelled North Central into the black.

For example, Carr fretted over the avalanche of customer complaints which were hangovers from the Morey administration. Carr soon established a policy of having every letter answered, complimentary or complaining, within one week. Each piece of correspondence still carries a reply deadline. For years, when incidents requiring investigation were relayed to the department concerned, Carr himself has reviewed the replies.

Buttomer, for a time, was one of the chief offenders inasmuch as he had a tendency to procrastinate. Carr finally ordered him to acknowledge every complaint promptly and prepare a memo telling Carr what the investigation showed and how the incident was being resolved. He occasionally overruled Buttomer and others—a rare exception to his no-interference policy—when it involved a passenger demand to be reimbursed for mishandled baggage.

Carr knew some of the damage and loss claims were inflated or outright phony, but he invariably agreed to pay at least part of the requested amount, with a letter that started out, "In an effort to retain your good will, we are sending you the enclosed check . . ."

Such a letter did *not* go to one passenger who complained that North Central had lost his "brand-new" suitcase. When it was finally located, the bag appeared to have been through World War II. After some checking was done, it turned out the suitcase had been manufactured by a firm that had gone out of business in 1926.

Dave Moran once got a note from Carr asking him to expedite recovery of a bag which a distraught passenger insisted was full of $250 suits, $50 shoes, $20 shirts and $9 ties. Moran found the luggage and opened it, anxious to see what $50 shoes looked like. The only contents were forty girlie magazines.

Carr's insistence on knowing what action was being taken to solve various problems was applied most effectively to the flight crews. One of his

Joe Louis, former world heavyweight boxing champion, flew from Milwaukee to Chicago on North Central.

first orders on taking over was to arrange for pilot discrepancy reports to be sent directly to him. He also wanted pilot complaints reported to him personally, before a mild gripe became a bitter hassle.

"Don't run around with it and just bitch," was his comment. "Write it down and let me do something about it."

He laid down another rule to Charlotte soon after she became his "alter ego," as one North Central official called her.

"If one of our pilots ever wants to see me, send him in immediately," he told her.

"Even if you're busy?" she asked doubtfully.

"Even if I'm busy. Look, the pilots know more about how the airline is running than anyone else—and I want to hear what they have to say."

On returning to North Central, Carr observed that the company seemed to be involved in a major battle with someone at nearly all of its cities. These included controversies with airport managers, city councils, politicians and newspapers.

One morning it occurred to him that the airline was at a disadvantage in these local disputes because it was always the outsider, and outsiders always lose.

"That's when it came to me," he recalls. "North Central's community relations could be greatly improved if the company could be represented by

President Hal Carr (standing, third from left) at a meeting with pilots in 1954. Shown are (seated, from left) Jack Jordan, Lloyd Franke, Fred Kremer, Chief Pilot Red Wallis, Pete Wahl and Bill Engelking; (standing) Lee Anderson, Operations Manager A. D. (Nemo) Niemeyer, Carr, Ray Ashley and Bob Murphy.

On October 21, 1954, Joseph Horner, Jr. was made a Presidential Advisor. The Business Manager of the Green Bay Press-Gazette received this certificate from North Central Stewardess Marna Jorgenson.

one or two leading citizens in every city it served, men who understood airline difficulties, say a banker, civic leader, newspaper editor—people with stature and good reputations."

From this idea evolved North Central's "Presidential Advisor" program which is not only effective public relations but, over the years, has proved to be of tremendous help to the company in solving many ticklish community situations. The group of Presidential Advisors is limited to 100 persons who serve as sounding boards to the airline in their communities and function as an informal Board of Directors.

The Presidential Advisor list includes corporation presidents, bankers, attorneys, newspaper publishers, and even one former Cabinet member, Secretary of Defense Melvin Laird, who was appointed a Presidential Advisor in 1955 when he was a Wisconsin Congressman.

The Presidential Advisors are unique in the airline industry. Other carriers have their "Admirals" and "Ambassadors," but the usual VIP designation is honorary. North Central's Advisors really work at their job, and are picked more for influence than affluence. From the very start, Carr believed in getting mileage out of every move—including the awarding of what could have been an empty title.

112

U. S. Representative Melvin R. Laird, Jr., of Marshfield,
Wisconsin was appointed a North Central Presidential Advisor
following his address before the Stevens Point Kiwanis Club
on September 13, 1955. Making the appointment were
Stewardesses JoAnn Borseth (left) and Nancy McGrouary.

On June 12, 1956, Wendell T. Burns, Senior Vice President of the
Northwestern National Bank of Minneapolis, was named a
Presidential Advisor. Making the presentation are Stewardesses
Connie Nelson (left) and Laura Campbell.

D. Clark Everest, Chairman of the Board, Marathon Corporation, Rothschild, Wisconsin, (center) was appointed a Presidential Advisor in his office on August 22, 1955. Attending were (from left) Arthur E. A. Mueller, North Central's Board Chairman; Stewardess Laura Campbell; Everest; Stewardess Sharon Vroman; and Presidential Advisor Walter Roehl, Executive Secretary of the Wausau Chamber of Commerce.

North Central employees soon became acquainted with Carr's refusal to "play President," as he put it, by demanding special treatment. He always insisted on standing in line with other North Central passengers to secure his ticket at the counter, even on crowded flights when the line was long.

He kept this rule inviolate until one time when a competing airline was on strike. Carr had to fly to Chicago and told Charlotte he would need to leave the office early because the counter would be jammed. Charlotte suggested that she get his ticket ahead of time so he could go directly to the gate. He declined. "No favors," he reminded her. "It's a favor to the other passengers," she remarked. "You'll save our agent's time with one less person to ticket." He gave in.

Later that day, Carr went to the terminal for his flight. Weaving between literally thousands of prospective passengers milling in the concourse, he finally reached the North Central gate. At least three people were "standing by" for each available seat, and nearly everyone seemed to have a dying relative or claimed to be a personal friend of the company's President. Most were edgy as they vied for passage. Suddenly, a bat swooped over the crowd. In the moment of silence that followed, somebody exclaimed, "I know they're using all the equipment they have, but if they try to put seats on that thing, I'm not going!" The tension broke.

By year's end, Carr was able to report one of the fastest and most remarkable comebacks in airline history. North Central had concluded 1953 with a net loss of $119,367. It wound up 1954 with a net profit of $80,222—and this despite a $139,764 reduction in mail pay. Operating costs per mile dipped from the regional airline high of $1.25 to 96 cents, which was 14 cents under the industry average. Even the winter months showed a profit, including November which had never before seen black ink. Furthermore, the swelling traffic shot North Central into first place among the then-thirteen regionals in number of passengers carried.

The CAB had finally come through with a permanent mail rate formula that varied with each airline's passenger load factor. North Central, with its unusually high load factor of 43.4 percent and total passenger count of nearly 284,000 (30 percent more than in 1953), drew one of the lowest mail pay rates in the industry. Carr wasn't unhappy, though; what had once constituted 83 percent of the airline's revenues was down to 40 percent. North Central had proof of what C. R. Smith, former American Airlines' President, once said about the DC-3: "It's the first airplane in history that can make money just carrying passengers."

North Central Secretary-Treasurer Bernard Sweet (left) greets General James H. (Jimmy) Doolittle, pioneer aviator and famed World War II pilot, during his 1955 visit to the airline. Looking on are Vice President-Maintenance and Engineering R. H. Bendio and (far right) A. D. Niemeyer, Vice President-Operations.

North Central's financial recovery in 1954 was given extensive coverage by the press.

The annual report, published in March of 1955, noted that traffic volume during January and February was 42 percent above the same two-month period for 1954.

"It is anticipated," Carr wrote, "that traffic will continue to gain throughout the year, and approximately 375,000 passengers will fly on North Central in 1955."

His estimate was conservative. The 1955 total was 430,445 passengers.

Carr also noted that in 1955 North Central made its first January profit ever—a "modest" $5,734 indicating "a trend toward a year-round self-sufficiency." He was conservative again. It was more than just a trend. The year 1955 was the most profitable in North Central's eight years of existence, showing a net of $98,000, and black ink every month. The payroll roster soared to 900 employees, and the eighteen-plane fleet increased to twenty with the purchase of two more DC-3s.

The additional equipment was badly needed to help operate new service introduced in 1955, including a lucrative route between Chicago and Detroit via South Bend, Kalamazoo, Battle Creek and Jackson. It was a typical Carr performance: North Central replaced American's two daily flights over this heavily industrialized route with six flights and eventually increased daily schedules to fourteen.

A huge crowd turned out in Kalamazoo, Michigan, for the inauguration of North Central's Chicago-Detroit flights on May 1, 1955. That day, the airline also began serving South Bend, Battle Creek and Jackson on this route.

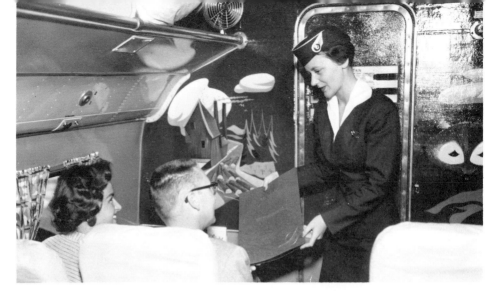

Vacationland scenes were painted on
the DC-3 cabin bulkheads in 1955.
Stewardess Mary Ogle (above, right)
offers a magazine to Operations
Secretary Donna Smith and Flight
Superintendent Lyle Ferguson on the
aircraft dubbed "Fox River Valley."
Captain William Engelking (right)
is shown on the DC-3 Northliner
named after the Mesabi Iron Range
country.

In 1955, reservationists at Milwaukee worked around a table. The
revolving center panels each represented a flight, and individual
reservations were inserted on cards. The room was located behind
the airport ticket counter.

Load factors rose sharply—from 43 percent to 50 percent, highest in the regional industry. On June 15, 1955, North Central carried a record 1,897 passengers in a single day; and two days later, the airline boarded its one-millionth passenger.

North Central was serving forty-three cities in six states—Wisconsin, Minnesota, North Dakota, Michigan, Illinois, and Indiana. On paper, the system looked great. But the company was handicapped by the inevitable operating restrictions placed on regional carriers. Routes between major cities had mandatory stops at smaller intermediate points, and no airline could make much money with this kind of pogo stick operation.

Carr readily conceded the importance of serving the smaller towns; this was the reason airlines like Wisconsin Central had come into existence. But he also knew the company would remain a relatively small potato, with no great potential earning capacity, without some nonstop authority.

A check for winnings in North Central's Maintenance Improvement Contest was presented (below) to Lead Mechanic Gordon King by R. H. Bendio, Vice President-Maintenance and Engineering. Also on hand were Mechanics Earl Jackson (left) and Joe Helgestad.

He received encouragement on May 19, 1955 when President Eisenhower signed into law a bill awarding all regional carriers permanent certificates. It was a tacit acknowledgment by the government that the industry had come of age and was now an integral part of the nation's air transportation system. Carr moved on three fronts:

1. He kept pushing for approval of the Lake Central merger, promising to increase service over Lake Central's system by 48 percent while saving the government a half-million dollars yearly in mail pay.

2. North Central aggressively pursued its applications in the CAB's "Seven States Area Investigation," a complex case relating to air service needs in the vast area stretching south and west of the company's system.

3. Carr applied for nonstop authority between the Twin Cities and Milwaukee, Madison-Chicago, and Twin Cities-Chicago.

The inaugural flight over the new Detroit-Chicago route arrived at Midway Airport on May 1, 1955. Special passengers included newspaper representatives from Jackson, Battle Creek, Kalamazoo, and South Bend and company officials. Standing in the doorway are First Officer Ray Kelly, President Hal Carr, Director G. F. DeCoursin, and Director Werner Christensen. In front of the stairs are Chief Stewardess Kathy Leddick and (continuing right) Chief Pilot G. F. (Red) Wallis and Stewardess Sharon Vroman.

Stewardess Dee Wisnauskas prepares to leave on a 1954 trip. Captain John Badger is in the DC-3 cockpit.

Awards in the company's new Idea Dollars program—for helpful suggestions that save money or improve operations—were given to employees. Two Twin Cities mechanics were among the 1955 winners. Electronics Superintendent Al Warner (left) presents a check to Radio Mechanic Robert Krause, while Line Maintenance Superintendent Robert Gren (right) congratulates Mechanic David Brown on his award.

121

This latter application brought Carr face-to-face with his predecessor, Howard Morey, who was in his old post as Chairman of the Wisconsin State Aeronautics Commission. Carr went before the Commission to ask for support of the nonstop Minneapolis/St. Paul-Chicago route. The group heard him out, and Morey suggested that Carr go back to his hotel and await their decision.

Carr waited from 4 p.m. to 8 p.m. with no word from Morey. He finally called Morey at home.

"Oh, sorry I didn't get back to you, Hal," Morey said nonchalantly. "The Commission voted not to support North Central's proposal."

Morey had his day, but Carr didn't waste time grieving over what he was convinced was pure vindictiveness. He was too busy filing more applications for new routes, including a proposed extension of the system beyond Detroit into Erie, Buffalo and Toronto. He also announced his intention of putting North Central in the helicopter business, filing for authority to provide helicopter service for the Detroit, Chicago-Milwaukee and the Twin Cities metropolitan areas. Subsequent applications for

A heavy Chicago rainfall sent these three North Central passengers off the ground ahead of their plane. They climbed aboard a settee in the flooded Chicago terminal on May 24, 1955, following a cloudburst and a temperature drop of 20 degrees in a single hour.

expanded helicopter operations were filed, but as it turned out, North Central was never to fly passenger-carrying "choppers". It would have been interesting to see if Carr's magic touch could have overcome the deficit-ridden tradition of helicopter airlines.

The North Central course reversal had a bright side effect. Eight cities on its routes (five of them served exclusively by North Central) began building modern terminals and improving runways. The annual report for 1955

Dramatizing North Central's soaring passenger traffic, Tariffs and Schedules Manager Chuck Vesper had to climb on a step ladder to plot June 1955 boardings.

rightly attributed this to "the security brought about by North Central's permanent status."

The report also contained this paragraph, worded with typical caution:

"More DC-3s will be added as required by increased traffic and route extensions. The company is also preparing for conversion to larger, faster aircraft when a suitable replacement for the DC-3 becomes available. An intensive program is underway to inspect and evaluate all possible replacements now offered and those being developed by the various aircraft manufacturers."

It was the first hint that Herman was finally getting ready to fly out of the DC-3 era.

President Hal Carr assists Miss Erika Faulkenberry, North Central's one-millionth passenger, after presenting her with roses. Miss Faulkenberry, a University of Wisconsin student, flew the "Route of the Northliners" on June 17, 1955.

124

CHAPTER SIX

En Route

Carr moved carefully. He wasn't ready to commit North Central to any expensive re-equipment program until it had routes and traffic capable of supporting larger aircraft.

For the next three years, the airline would pursue those twin goals relentlessly while little Herman had to be satisfied with his DC-3s. In 1956, North Central increased its fleet to twenty-four planes that flew nearly 100 flights a day—an operation involving a takeoff or landing every ninety seconds. The passenger total was 551,775, somewhat less than what Carr had projected for the year. The poorer-than-expected showing was due to four months of particularly severe winter weather.

Net profit after taxes dipped to $10,691 that year. North Central and other regional airlines complained that the Civil Aeronautics Board's new permanent mail rate didn't deserve the adjective "permanent," mostly because it hindered expansion and failed to provide for stiffer income taxes. The CAB agreed to set a new and higher rate.

The Lake Central merger was up in the air. In June of 1956, a CAB examiner recommended approval, but strong opposition had developed sometime ago in the form of a lawsuit filed by the Lake Central Employee Stockholder Group. They claimed North Central had violated the original purchase agreement by filing a separate application for Lake Central's routes and by deliberately delaying CAB proceedings on the case.

North Central said the purchase agreement authorized the application for Lake Central's routes and denied that it had sought to delay the case. North Central did, it conceded, ask the CAB for brief postponements on two or three occasions, but on five others it moved for expedited hearings.

*Captain Robert Ceronsky (left), Stewardess Nancy McGrouary and
First Officer Richard O'Neill approach their DC-3 Northliner in
front of the terminal at Minneapolis-St. Paul International Airport
in 1956.*

Actually, the case had been delayed when the CAB expanded the merger
hearings into a sweeping investigation of the overall service in Lake
Central's area. The CAB took this action after Allegheny and Ozark also
applied for Lake Central's routes and turned the merger case into a
donnybrook. As it turned out, none of the route applications ever reached
the hearing stage, and the CAB considered the merger case exclusively.

On September 20, 1956, the U.S. District Court in Indianapolis declared
the contract to be invalid. The airline appealed to the U.S. Seventh Circuit
Court of Appeals in Chicago, and the CAB deferred any merger decision
pending the outcome. On March 5, 1957, the Chicago court upheld North
Central's appeal by ruling that the contract was legally enforceable.

A week later, the CAB handed North Central a fat award: a new route
from Grand Forks to Omaha via Fargo, North Dakota; Watertown,
Brookings, Sioux Falls and Yankton, South Dakota; Sioux City, Iowa; and
Norfolk, Nebraska. This added eight cities, three new states and 579 miles
to the system.

However, the Appeals Court victory proved meaningless. On July 9, the
CAB turned thumbs down on the merger on the grounds that the routes
served by the two carriers were not complementary trade areas and, if

merged, would create a local service system of unprecedented size. Carr was disappointed, but far from heartbroken, inasmuch as the company was gaining—through normal route applications—more territory than it would have obtained if the Lake Central merger had been approved.

Those applications poured into the CAB so fast that at one time Carr figured the CAB would be handing down at least one decision affecting North Central every ninety days. By the end of 1957, the company had proposals before the CAB that, if approved, would have expanded the

President Hal Carr points out North Central's growth to Milwaukee Presidential Advisor Robert Hamilton, President of The Dumore Company (at right) during the airline's Eighth Anniversary activities in Milwaukee.

North Central celebrated its Eighth Anniversary with a reception at Milwaukee in February 1956. Representing the eight years (and 1956) are (from right) Stewardesses Nancy McGrouary, Joyce Forrest, Laura Campbell, Connie Nelson, Sharon Vroman, Margaret Jerome, JoAnn Borseth, Sherry Nighsonger, and Gail Anderson.

Wayne W. Parrish, President of American Aviation Publications, pauses with Stewardess Shirley Skarpness on the steps of a North Central DC-3. Parrish, well-known aviation editor and publisher, visited the airline on a trip through the Twin Cities in 1956.

Former President Harry S. Truman arrived in Chicago on a North Central DC-3 in September 1956.

General Office personnel joined station managers at their 1956 annual meeting. Seated are (from left) Jeanne Maley, Carol Kallunki, Dorothy Akre, Peggy Witherell, Bob Baker, Kathy Leddick, Maggie Fogarty and Charlotte Westberg. Standing are (from left) Dave Moran, Robert Bruemmer (TWA interline representative), Brad Teasdale, Marv Freund, Clyde Sundberg, Ed Noga, Chet Matthews, Bernard Sweet, Jim Butala, Joe Sims, Tom Christensen, Harry House, Jim Perry, Ray Miller (in front), Frank Buttomer, Gordon Holemo, Bob Erdmann, Tom Needham, Frank Seitz, Don Sonnichsen, Charlie Cox, Ken Schuck, Red Behling, Hal Carr, Gene Kacner, Kent Kistler, Newt Ragan, and John O'Keefe.

Stewardess JoAnn Borseth (right) was named "Miss Spirit of St. Louis" in 1957. From among 1,200 nominees and 39 finalists, she was judged to be the "World's Ideal Airline Stewardess." Nancee Parkinson, (photo left, with her father, Captain Ralph Parkinson) was chosen "Miss Minnesota" in 1961 and became a top runner-up in the Miss America contest that year.

system from 53 cities in nine states to 178 cities in 16 states, plus three Canadian provinces. The additional routes totaled more than 11,000 miles, enough to have made North Central the nation's largest scheduled carrier in terms of route mileage.

Not all were granted, of course, and Carr was temporarily satisfied to keep North Central at the top of the regional airline standings in passengers boarded—680,930 in 1957 and 777,140 in 1958. The year 1957, which marked the company's tenth year of scheduled service, saw total employees rise to 1,250 and the DC-3 fleet expand to twenty-seven air- craft. In April, the airline carried its two-millionth passenger; it had taken eight years to reach the one-million mark, but only two years to hit the second million.

Another 1957 success was recorded by a North Central stewardess, JoAnn Borseth. Competing against 1,200 nominees and thirty-nine finalists, she was named "Miss Spirit of St. Louis," the World's Ideal Airline Stewardess. (A second member of the North Central family was honored in the pulchritude field when Captain Ralph Parkinson's daughter Nancee became Miss Minnesota of 1961 and went on to be a top runner-up in the Miss America contest.)

To acknowledge outstanding performance, a "Station of the Year" program was instituted. The first award was received by the Green Bay station for 1956. Manager Robert Smith (right) accepts the citation from Vice President-Traffic and Sales Frank Buttomer. Secretary Florence Kalackas holds a duplicate plaque to be displayed in the station; the other was for "Smitty" personally. Chicago Reservations-Space Control also earned "Station of the Year" honors for 1956. Superintendent of Reservations/Ticketing Marvin Freund (left) accepts the plaque from Buttomer.

Duluth was the site of North Central's Ninth Anniversary reception in 1957. From left are Stewardess Emily Ferguson, City Attorney Richard Bye, Chamber of Commerce Manager Robert Morris (North Central Presidential Advisor), Chief Stewardess Kathy Leddick, President Hal Carr, Airport Manager Earl Olson (Presidential Advisor), Stewardess Laura Campbell and KDAL-TV President Dalton LeMasurier (Presidential Advisor).

If North Central was still a DC-3 airline (with the jet age only a year away), Carr made sure it was the best DC-3 operation in the industry. "Station of the Year" awards were started; Green Bay and Chicago Reservations Control were first to receive the coveted bronze plaques.

A "Crew of the Year" program was inaugurated to honor pilots and stewardesses; and the first awards went to Captain Lee Molbreak, First Officer Richard Wagner and Stewardess Patricia Sweet of Madison; Captain Charles Nason, First Officer Daniel Pruss and Stewardess Bette Ward of Chicago; Captain Oak Mackey, First Officer Ronald Kielty and Stewardess Robbie Apitz of Detroit; Captain Duane Petit, First Officer Robert Krueger and Stewardess Joan Alexander of Minneapolis.

May of 1957 saw the beginning of a project to improve the appearance of all stations and offices. It was dubbed "Operation Sparkle" and won general industry acclaim. Little Herman was not only becoming an outstanding airline, it was beginning to look like one.

Carr also was getting help from North Central's "family"—more than half the cities on the system had major airport improvements underway, all scheduled for completion by the end of 1958 and involving everything from new terminals to longer runways with instrument landing systems.

Public support was being expressed in more ways than better airports, for North Central actually was becoming competitive with the trunk airlines at key points. At Milwaukee, for example, during one summer month North Central boarded more passengers than any other airline. This

Vice President-Traffic and Sales Frank Buttomer takes a reservation much to the delight of Passenger Service Agents Marilyn Johnson (left) and Joline Orley. Buttomer had promised to toss a "genuine wingding" for the entire staff if North Central placed first in passengers among the six airlines serving Milwaukee. It happened in July 1956. On the day of the party, Buttomer imported officers and management people from over the system to run the station so everyone could attend. Besides working the evening shift, which regaled partygoers who stopped by, the "recruits" opened up the next morning.

was the first time a regional carrier had ever surpassed a trunk at a major terminal, and it was no temporary achievement; North Central still is the dominant carrier at Milwaukee.

Civic loyalty was demonstrated when the CAB held hearings on North Central's application to provide Duluth/Superior with nonstop service to Chicago, Milwaukee, Madison and Green Bay. In 1952, Northwest Airlines' Duluth-Chicago service, via Minneapolis/St. Paul, had been temporarily suspended and turned over to North Central—but with a requirement that four stops be made between Duluth and Chicago. A parade of civic witnesses went before the CAB to urge permanent suspension of Northwest, and this marked the first time a metropolitan area had ever gone on record to support a regional airline over a trunk to the point of totally excluding the latter.

Personnel and planes kept pace with the route expansion. Employees totaled 1,400 by the end of 1958, and the DC-3 fleet now numbered thirty-two—making North Central the nation's largest operator of the famed transport. Once more, the company led the other twelve regionals in all classes of traffic—passengers, charter revenue, air mail and express.

The charter business was beginning to provide some hefty income. It didn't really start until 1956, but in that one year North Central carried more than 2,000 passengers on 113 charter trips—including one of the airline's most unusual passengers. She was a wealthy, elderly woman who lived in Brainerd, Minnesota, and liked to spend her winters in Tucson, Arizona. Every winter for several years, she chartered a North Central DC-3 for herself, her dog, and a traveling companion to make the trip.

These stewardess graduates received their "wings" from President Hal Carr at March 1957 ceremonies. From left are Mary Griffel, Diane McConnell, Phyllis Bolly, Marlene Shipman, LaVerne Noga, Harriet Peacock, Mavis Thompson, Florence Bashista, Bonnie Hermsen, Sharon Davenport and Chief Stewardess Kathy Leddick.

A "Crew of the Year" program was initiated in 1960. Award winners from each of the airline's four domiciles were chosen by their fellow flight crew members. In Minneapolis/St. Paul, President Hal Carr presented certificates to First Officer Robert Krueger, Stewardess Joan Alexander and Captain Duane (Pete) Petit.

First Officer Richard Wagner (left), Stewardess Patricia Sweet and Captain Lee Molbreak earned 1960 "Crew of the Year" honors in Madison.

Chicago chose First Officer Daniel Pruss (left), Stewardess Bette Ward and Captain Charles Nason as its first "Crew of the Year."

President Hal Carr (second from right) met with Detroit's 1960 "Crew of the Year," First Officer Ronald Kielty (left), Stewardess Robbie Apitz and Captain Oak Mackey.

She always insisted on the same stewardess. Jan Kinna had worked the first Brainerd-Tucson charter, and at the lady's request, was assigned to all the subsequent ones.

"I remember she always brought along her own food," Jan says, "and it was something. Caviar to her was a staple, which should give you an idea of how I was living it up on those flights."

Step by step, improvement by improvement, innovation by innovation, the airline grew. The three-millionth passenger boarded August 26, 1958, only sixteen months after the two-million mark had been reached. To meet the needs of the mushrooming traffic, the company's reservations system was modernized to the point of efficiently handling up to 125,000 passengers a month. Another project was North Central's telephone courtesy program for employees with public contact duties. Carr hired two speech experts who traveled all over the system teaching better diction, improved telephone techniques, and correct speech. They never did succeed in reforming Charlie Cox completely, but otherwise the plan was a success.

In August 1958, North Central boarded a record 76,011 passengers—the greatest number ever carried by a regional airline in a single month. The total was 32,000 more than the company had hauled in its first two years and not much less than the total for the first three years.

But passenger boardings were not North Central's big news for that year. On December 9, the Civil Aeronautics Board issued its long-awaited final decision in the Seven States Area Investigation. Carr didn't get everything he asked for, but he got plenty: 2,000 additional route miles and eighteen

President Hal Carr (center) hosted State Representative Francis LaBrosse (left) and State Senator Gordon Butler, both of Duluth, at the opening of North Central's new city ticket office in the Hotel Duluth on November 30, 1957.

Eighteen new stewardesses are graduated in February 1959 and
accept congratulations from company officers. From left are Vice
President-Maintenance and Engineering R. H. Bendio, Katherine
Karnstedt, Selma Wald, Sharon Jensen, Rosemary Plummer, Coral
Zeleznikar, Doris Zehringer, Muriel Hewitt, Bonnie Kehoe, Vice
President-Operations A. D. Niemeyer, Barbara Peterson, Barbara
Kress, Margo Scheller, Norma Turner, Alice Nugent, Vice
President-Traffic and Sales Frank Buttomer, Barbara Mueller, Lizzi
Schwanke, Jewel Brueckner, Deborah Johnson, Jean Brock and
Secretary-Treasurer Bernard Sweet.

Accepting a handsome copper plaque from Harold Sage on behalf of
North Central is Charlotte Westberg, assistant to President Hal
Carr. The plaque was a gift to Carr from Presidential Advisors Sage
and John Rice of Houghton, Michigan. The presentation was made
at the new Houghton County Airport terminal dedication in 1958.

Ceremonies were held at all points along the route when Grand
Forks-Omaha service was inaugurated in 1957. Among those
participating at Norfolk, Nebraska, were (from left) Stewardess
JoAnn Borseth ("Miss Spirit of St. Louis"), South Dakota Governor
Joe Foss, North Central President Hal Carr and Director Kenneth B.
Willett (background), Nebraska Governor Victor Anderson and
North Dakota Lt. Governor Clyde Duffy.

To climax North Central's Tenth Anniversary, the first "Pioneer
Banquet" was held on March 7, 1958 in Minneapolis. Considered
"pioneers" are those currently employed who were with the company
when scheduled operations began on February 24, 1948. Seated are
(from left) George Bell, Milton Ellyson, Francis Van Hoof, Charles
Nason, Lloyd Franke, Robert Ceronsky, Walter Kneller, Kenneth
Sersland, Jack Starry, George Roycraft, Peter Hofman, G. F.
DeCoursin, William Yunker, Ralph Parkinson, and Matt Ruper.
Standing left to right, are Myron Broten, Robert Allison, Gale
Lorsbach, Gordon Torkelson, Duane Petit, Harold Ebelt, Earl
Barron, Fred Kremer, Alexander Banks, Robert Swennes, Arthur
Hinke, Hal Carr, Robert Gren, Herbert Splettstoeser, Joseph Dick,
Hal Picquet, Raymond Miller, Frank Seitz, Joseph Sims, Charles
Cox, Oscar Malotky, Donald Planck, Kenneth Schuck, Thomas
Needham, Richard Cooper, Arthur Schwandt and Robert Smith.
(Not shown are Ray Ashley, Magnus Budzien, John Downing and
James Grant.)

new cities. The decision swelled North Central's routes to more than 5,000 miles and communities served to sixty-five in nine states.

Carr wasted no time. He already had authority—voted by the stockholders eight months earlier—to negotiate two loans totaling $7.5 million. He also had the benefit of a Federal law that guaranteed 90 percent of the amount a regional airline had to borrow for new aircraft. Armed with this double-barrelled financial support, he went shopping for airplanes.

Carr was, is and always will be enormously deliberate in aircraft selection, saying, "One of the worst mistakes an airline can make is to buy the wrong airplane." He had held out against DC-3s in the early days of Wisconsin Central, knowing they were too expensive to buy and operate over a system that could only partially accommodate them. He had then resisted phasing out the DC-3s until he had routes and traffic for larger planes. Now, at last, he was ready—but still cautious.

The F-27, a twin-engine turboprop being built by Fairchild, was available. It was the first aircraft specifically designed to meet short-haul airline requirements, and Carr was attracted. North Central had never had a new plane, and his fellow feeder executives were ordering the F-27 in large numbers. Particularly intriguing was the prospect of operating a jet-powered aircraft. But Carr also examined the price tag of $1 million, the relatively limited seating capacity of forty, and the equally limited cargo space.

Carr continued looking and came up with a prize. Continental had five Convair 340s for sale. After lengthy negotiations with Bob Six, Continental's president, Carr got the price down to $325,000 apiece and

Regional Chief Pilot Milt Ellyson prepares to cut a piece of Tenth Anniversary cake in Chicago for Base Stewardess Supervisor Emily Ferguson (left) and Stewardess Diane McConnell. In 1958, North Central carried its three-millionth passenger and received 2,000 additional route miles in the Seven States Area Investigation.

137

North Central selected Convair 340s to replace the DC-3s. The first five were purchased in 1959 from Continental Air Lines.

Richard M. Nixon chartered a North Central DC-3 in the Fall of 1964 to make a campaign speech in Mankato, Minnesota.

Vice President of Flight Operations A. D. Niemeyer (left) and Regional Chief Pilot Arthur Hinke inspect the cockpit of North Central's first Convair 340 in 1959.

snapped them up. It cost another $80,000 each to refurbish them, but the $405,000 per airplane was more than a half-million dollars under what an F-27 would have been. Furthermore, the Convairs carried forty-four passengers, and their cargo space was greater than the Fairchild's. It seemed more important than boasting about "going jet."

A former Fairchild official, privy to North Central's consideration of the F-27, recalls that Carr made quite an impression on him at the time.

"We kept trying to sell him on the desirability of keeping up with the regionals buying turbine aircraft," he says. "Carr couldn't have cared less. His philosophy was that an airline shouldn't have fancy, glamorous new equipment just for the sake of bragging about it—what counted to him was the way a carrier operated its equipment and treated its passengers. Damned if he didn't halfway convince me, as badly as we wanted to sell the F-27 to what obviously was the biggest and best regional airline in the country."

Carr borrowed, from various lenders, $2.34 million to finance the Convair purchase. The company also arranged for a $2-million working capital loan, and this made the stockholders happy because both notes combined were $3 million less than they had authorized. The five new planes gave North Central a fleet of thirty-seven aircraft, but Carr already was planning to phase out the DC-3s. He scheduled the Convairs mostly on segments granted in the Seven States award; half of the eighteen new points had formerly been served by Braniff and Western, and he didn't want to downgrade service by putting in DC-3s.

Karl Brocken was handed a new assignment—doll up the new airplanes and the old ones as well. Brocken came up with a design that called for royal blue, stretched-out lettering of "NORTH CENTRAL" over the line of windows, thin red stripes running the length of the fuselage, a red feather motif extending back from the cockpit windows, and a large "Herman" on the tail. He proposed something else to Carr.

"Paint the top of the fuselage white," he suggested.

"Why?" Carr asked.

"Better heat-reflecting qualities. I tried it once on a Capital DC-4 a few years ago. On a hot day, it lowered cabin temperatures by as much as 15 degrees. It costs a little more to maintain, but it's worth it if you want more passenger comfort."

"I'll buy it," Carr said.

It took more than 4,000 man-hours to ready each Convair for service. All five Convairs were equipped with weather radar, an added safety feature which also improved passenger comfort. In addition, the aircraft had galleys that allowed the company to introduce specialty snacks for short hops and hot meal service on the long hauls. The industry's first "beer flights" were inaugurated that summer over selected North Central routes.

To oversee the food service, Carr promoted a young man named George Karnas who was a senior station agent in Duluth/Superior and a union representative at the time. Art Schwandt was impressed with his conduct during labor negotiations and recommended him to Carr. Karnas, in turn, had been impressed by North Central's President, who believed that all differences of opinion could somehow be resolved equitably. (Carr later settled a contract by betting the union negotiator he could do fifty pushups. The burly negotiator, examining Carr's rather slight build, snorted, "If you can do fifty, I'll sign." He signed.)

Twenty-one stewardesses were graduated in the first Convair-era class in April 1959. From left, front row, are Therese Delia, Phyllis Sterling, Anne Supalla, Virginia Reynolds, Roberta Seuferer, Nancy Tresh, Carole Gossage, Nancy Murphy, Donna Wick; (top left, on airstair) Toni Cirimotich, Judith Planer, Kay Kivel, Harriet Irons, Barbara Frank and Edith Porter; (top right) Caroline Sullivan, Marilyn Lynch, Mary Ihnet, Fay Rostollan, Nancy Carufel and Juanita Casteel.

The airline industry's first "Beer Flights" were launched by North Central in 1959. Stewardess Lizzi Schwanke performed the christening ceremonies in Milwaukee from atop an oldtime Pabst Blue Ribbon beer wagon.

In the first year of food service, Karnas spent only $27,000, (it's now over $3 million annually.) He started with an assistant, a part-time secretary and an immediate headache—he had bought 3,000 aircraft serving trays and lost them all in one week. They were gray, the same color as Braniff's, and the Minneapolis caterer kept putting them on Braniff planes.

The stewardesses greeted the Convairs like a Cessna pilot would welcome a sudden assignment to 747s. The bigger planes meant an end to the relatively idyllic life of a DC-3 cabin attendant, as far as inflight duties were concerned. Training now had to be stepped up in every area from service to safety. The day Jan Kinna took her first Convair trip, she gaped at the forty-four passengers, remembered how easy it was with only twenty-one and no meal service, and burst into tears.

"I just didn't see how I could serve forty-four people with beer and pretzels in thirty-five minutes," she explains.

With the introduction of the Convair 340 "Super Northliner," the fleet was given a new exterior design. The 44-passenger, pressurized, radar-equipped aircraft cruises at 284 miles per hour, enabling North Central pilots to fly above the weather for the first time.

Joan Northern Livingston believes passenger attitudes began changing with the advent of the Convairs, and eventually, even more with the jets.

"In the early days," she theorizes, "they were just glad to get where they were going. Once they flew in a little more luxury, they became more demanding. It had to happen, of course; but sometimes as I look back on my DC-3 days when a stew's life was so simple, it's easy to forget all the discomfort."

Pilots traditionally fall in love with new airplanes—with reservations, and North Central's crews were no exception. Generally, they liked the Convair 340. It was fast—284 MPH cruising speed at 20,000 feet compared with 160 for the DC-3. Pressurization gave North Central's pilots their first chance to fly above the weather. The Convair's range was over 2,000 miles, while the DC-3's was 900. It also was one of the first airliners to have a power-operated integral airstair door, which meant faster boarding and deplaning.

The 340 was an uncomplaining, exceptionally stable airplane, "with no bad habits," as one pilot put it. It handled well in the stiffest crosswind, and aileron control was smoothly responsive even near stall speed. Some of the DC-3 veterans, who had been complaining for years that the old bird climbed like a motorized bathtub and handled like a rusty bulldozer, voiced doubts about the Convair—too fast, they groused, the wing was too stiff and the controls too light. But they were in the minority. While the Convair never earned the nostalgic affection bestowed on the DC-3, it is probably the best all-around piston-engine airliner ever built.

There wasn't any doubt that the 340 was an immediate success on North Central. The Convairs, dubbed "Super Northliners," began flying the system April 26, 1959. Operating inexperience with the bigger planes gave

142

the "We'll-Always-Love-The-Threes" contingent a crowing opportunity: the 340s flew 95.6 percent of their scheduled mileage, while the DC-3s operated 97.2 percent of theirs. The daily utilization for the DC-3s in 1959 was seven hours and twenty minutes, highest in the local airline industry; and the Convairs averaged six and a half hours. The lower utilization rate, however, stemmed largely from the fact that the Convairs were flying longer-haul segments at faster speeds. Their most important contribution to North Central was their drastically lower seat-mile cost.

Non-recurring expense items kept North Central's 1959 profits down to $32,697. Route development charges were one; the ill-fated Lake Central merger case alone drained North Central of over $100,000. To handle the Convairs, a new $350,000 maintenance hangar was built near the company's quarters at the Twin Cities' Wold-Chamberlain Field. It included offices for the Maintenance and Engineering department and for Schwandt's Industrial Relations department.

Training costs also zoomed with the introduction of Convairs. North Central leased a building adjacent to the airport to house a new Training Center. A third building acquired at the time was located across from the maintenance hangar, and this one-story structure provided space for the Chief Engineer and his staff.

It was a jerry-built arrangement at best, and seeds were planted in Carr's never-idle mind: someday, he mused, North Central would need a brand-new facility capable of housing all functions under one roof. It was to take another ten years before that particular dream was realized.

The airline's first Training Center, opened in 1959, was housed in this former school building located near the company's headquarters at the Minneapolis-St. Paul International Airport.

Lead Mechanic William B. Yunker (left), one of North Central's original employees, became the first to retire on July 31, 1959. He accepts "thanks and best wishes" from Vice President of Industrial Relations Arthur Schwandt.

North Central became an "international" airline when service was extended to Port Arthur/Fort William (now Thunder Bay) in Ontario, Canada, on December 1, 1960. Participating in inaugural ceremonies were (from left) Orv Wieben, fixed base operator at Fort William; North Central's Vice President of Traffic and Sales Frank Buttomer, Manager of Public Relations Donald Wright, President Hal Carr; and Port Arthur Mayor Norman Wilson.

144

Acquisition of the five Convairs pushed North Central's available seat miles up a whopping 35 percent. Traffic was nearing the one-million-a-year-mark—957,751 passengers were carried in 1959, and Carr wasn't afraid to butt heads with the giants. On the Milwaukee-Chicago segment, for example, North Central was competing against American and Northwest with fifty-four daily flights—a mass scheduling policy that paid off by garnering 85 percent of the market. It worked even in the smaller cities. Oshkosh, with seven daily flights, was averaging only three passengers per flight until Carr jumped the schedules to fourteen a day. The average passenger load per flight went up to more than five a day. The same thing happened at Duluth/Superior, where ten daily flights averaged only five passengers each. An increase to twenty-four flights still produced better than seven passengers per flight.

There were some mutterings in the lower echelons to the effect that the fleet was being over-scheduled. Carr's tart response: "Airplanes don't make money sitting on the ground."

Integration of the Convairs into the system was fast and efficient, so much so that Carr already was planning to buy more Convairs. He had service authorized to points in Ontario and Saskatchewan, Canada, that would make North Central the first regional airline to operate international routes. And he was thinking beyond the piston-engine aircraft—to the age of jet power. In his desk was a carefully-studied report showing that a Convair converted into a turboprop had a potential earnings increase of $200,000 a year based on a higher block speed of fifty miles per hour, annual utilization of 2,500 hours, and a revenue rate of eight cents a mile.

Again, he bided his time, concentrating more on day-to-day growth, rather than grandiose schemes for the future. In 1960, the airline topped the one-million mark in passengers carried. The total was 1,035,076, which happened to be one-sixth of what the entire thirteen-carrier regional industry boarded that year. And never before had a regional airline flown one million passengers. Ninety cities were now on North Central's routes, and only giant United served more. In August, the CAB handed down its decision in the Great Lakes Area Investigation, and Herman spread his wings ever wider.

The Great Lakes ruling gave North Central another 1,267 route miles in the heart of Michigan's industrial center and added Cleveland to the system. Service was inaugurated into Canada at Port Arthur/Fort William, Ontario, and a route from Minot, North Dakota, to Regina, Saskatchewan, was opened a few months later.

Daily passenger traffic was running more than 50 percent ahead of Allegheny, the nation's second largest regional line. Another monthly

Oshkosh earned "Station of the Year" honors in 1960. From left are (front row) Burt Moe, Vern Neubert, Manager Al Jaeger, Russ Desotell and Louis Griedl; (second row) Bonnie Seifeldt, Everett Ellestad, Pete Webber, Nancy Glidden and Donna Steffen; (third row) Jeannie Terrace, Judy Manney, Darlene Hampton and Harry Nielsen; (fourth row) Freda Dieterlen, Don Arne, Ann Bartol, Jerry Beckman and Jim McKay.

Aberdeen also won "Station of the Year" honors for 1960. Present for the plaque presentation were (front row, from left) Director of Ground Operations Thomas Needham; Mrs. Janice Boysen; Mrs. Colleen Renoos; Station Manager Norm Renoos; Barbara Hoffman; Superintendent of Stations Robert Baker; second row, Regional Superintendent Richard Cooper; Agent Dean Click; Agent Paul Hauck; Chicago District Station Manager and former Aberdeen Manager John Holland; and Agents Darwyn Boysen, Walter Achterberg, Duane Heng, Floyd Weieneth, and Harlan Lea.

record fell in August when North Central boarded 101,705 passengers. Carr ordered five more Convairs of the 340/440 series (the 440 was an improved model) after borrowing $2.45 million from the Irving Trust Company of New York and the Northwestern National Bank of Minneapolis. The fact that one of New York City's biggest banks saw fit to invest in North Central's future showed how far Carr had brought the airline in only seven years.

The loan was just one of his moves to strengthen the airline's financial status during 1960. North Central offered nearly 43,000 shares of common stock to its stockholders on a pro rata basis and to employees on a seniority basis. The offering was fully subscribed, adding $300,000 to working capital and 600 employees as new stockholders.

Revenues reached a high of almost $22 million. Bud Sweet, who was now Vice President and Secretary-Treasurer, brought in the final figures for the year. Carr could only shake his head in proud nostalgia. He remembered that when Wisconsin Central had been formed, grossing even $1 million a year seemed like a wild dream.

Carr frequently refused offers to head other companies because they were "too damn big"—perhaps not realizing that he was doing everything in his power to cause North Central to grow even larger than the firms wooing him.

Managerial changes and personnel shifts were other weapons to keep North Central prepared for its rapid expansion. Chief Pilot Wallis was promoted to Manager of Flight Operations under Niemeyer who, in turn,

Gold wings for stewardesses with five years of service in 1960 were presented by President Hal Carr and Chief Stewardess Kathy Leddick. From left are Nancy Nielsen, JoAnn Borseth, Carmen Tucker, Carr, Marge White, Joan Alexander and Miss Leddick.

had been upped to Vice President-Flight Operations. Carr talked one of the industry's top Convair maintenance experts, Leslie J. Keely, into leaving Braniff and put him directly under Bendio, now Vice President-Maintenance and Engineering. With the Convair fleet swelling, the post of Supervisor of Flight Training was established. Station supervisory personnel were realigned, two new regional superintendents were appointed, and the entire station system was reorganized into four regions—western, central, northern and eastern.

Buttomer, his days of shoestring operations over, had an enlarged sales force going gung-ho for new business—North Central's sales staff, for example, made almost 15,000 personal sales visits in 1960 and kept increasing that figure each year.

One day, Carr got a call from the North Central Master Executive Council of the Air Line Pilots Association. The pilots invited him to a little party, using the occasion to present him with an award for his "keen interest in pilot opinion" which "contributes immeasurably to the high morale and excellent company-pilot working relationship." Carr, a licensed pilot himself, was especially touched and rightfully so.

Pilots of many airlines have been traditionally "anti-management" since the days when ALPA was formed and pilots had to hold their union meetings in secret for fear a company would fire them if their membership were known. This feeling was never the case in North Central's close-knit family, and Carr was pleased with the airmen's gesture.

More records fell in 1961 ...

—The eighth consecutive year of profitable operations, with a net of $204,300.

On behalf of North Central's pilots, Captain Del Hendrickson, Jr. (right) presents President Hal Carr with an award for his "keen interest in pilot opinion" and for fostering "the excellent company-pilot working relationship."

148

Flight Operations Vice President A. D. (Nemo) Niemeyer (left) and Manager G. F. (Red) Wallis hang up another National Safety Council award for display. The 1960 plaque marked the thirteenth consecutive year that North Central operated without a fatality or injury to passengers or crew members.

—1,095,859 passengers carried, 30 percent more than the local service runner-up.

—4,285 passengers carried on June 16, a new record for a single day.

—112,111 passengers boarded in one month, August.

—The fourteenth consecutive National Safety Council award for a perfect safety record, which by now added up to 6.4 million passengers carried and over one billion passenger miles flown without an injury or fatality.

—Just under 16 million pounds of cargo and 6.5 million pounds of mail, the latter volume being 83 percent more than the second-ranked local service airline flew.

A new $1.25-million hangar went up at Chicago's O'Hare Field, fast becoming a major North Central station. The airline had started serving O'Hare in 1959 with three daily departures and a total of less than 6,000 passengers enplaned for the year. What was to become the nation's busiest airport ranked only twenty-fifth among North Central's stations. By the start of 1961, schedules had been increased to eighteen daily departures, and the 52,000 passengers carried had sent O'Hare to fourth place on the system.

Carr started establishing a DC-3 phase-out program. His timetable called for acquiring five to seven Convairs a year until all the "Threes" could be retired. The first two DC-3s were sold in 1961, and the Convair fleet went up to ten. North Central floated another equipment loan through

President Hal Carr (right) presents plaques to members of the Minneapolis/St. Paul "Crew of the Year" for 1961. They are (from left) Captain Lee Anderson, Stewardess Nancy Abrahamson and First Officer LeRoy Bauer.

Flight personnel in Chicago selected Stewardess Muriel Hewitt, Captain James Beyer (seated) and First Officer John Zimmer for "Crew of the Year" honors in 1961.

Detroit's 1961 "Crew of the Year" members are First Officer Foster Green (left), Stewardess Dorothy Korney and Captain Jim Hanson.

150

the Irving Trust and Northwestern National Bank—this one for nearly $2.9 million. The transaction was significant; it was consummated without use of the Federal guaranteed loan program.

The growth pattern remained the same for the next five years. More traffic, more route applications, more planes—and ever-present cost control. It was typical that North Central continued to expand in every area except number of employees. The payroll hovered around the 2,000 level between 1960 and 1966, and twice—in '61 and '63—actually dipped below that mark.

Year by year, the story was a familiar one:

1962—Eight more Convair 440s added with no DC-3 retirements . . . 99 percent of scheduled mileage flown and an on-time performance of 81 percent for nearly 190,000 flight arrivals . . . more than one million passengers for the third consecutive year . . . a record net profit of $439,940 . . . the fifteenth consecutive Safety Council Award.

1963—Another profit year of over $500,000 . . . a record 1.2 million passengers flown . . . another perfect safety record . . . a scheduled mileage completion rate that was third best among the country's twenty-four airlines.

1964—The Convair fleet increased to twenty-four and the DC-3 fleet reduced to eighteen . . . 1.3 million passengers boarded . . . the largest net

North Central's sales staff held its 1962 meeting in Minneapolis/ St. Paul. Attending were (from left) Jim Palm, Steve Haugen, Bill Domres, Bob Peck, Gene Leonard, Wayne Harris, Jim Thompson, Warren Rowe, Marv Fritz, Tim Grote, Tom Amburn, Jon Harty, Tom Cooper, Don LaMont, Henry Thiele, Manager of Sales Administration John Hammer and Bob Shook.

profit in North Central's history: $844,564 ... a new nonstop route between Pierre and Huron, South Dakota.

1965—Net profit topped $1.1 million, passengers carried rose to 1.6 million ... Convairs now at thirty and the DC-3 fleet down to sixteen, with Convairs flying 90 percent of North Central's seat miles.

1966—The second straight million-dollar profit year ... the two-million passenger mark reached for the first time . . . thirty-one Convairs and fifteen DC-3s in the fleet . . . the nineteenth consecutive National Safety Council Award.

Cold figures, however, can never tell the whole story; one must backtrack a bit.

There was "Operation Cold Front," for example. North Central operates under severe winter weather conditions longer than any other carrier in the country. Unfavorable weather plagues the airline six months out of the year. Yet the company consistently achieves excellent schedule performance in the face of handicaps that would daunt a polar bear—and it isn't done with mirrors or through the power of prayer.

Operation Cold Front was developed in 1961 and went into full-scale implementation the following year, with a five-step standardized program for every station on the system:

1. Snow removal requirements were set with each airport manager.

2. All airport equipment was to be winterized by September 15.

3. A plan was designed for inspection, care and periodic testing of all winter equipment.

4. Preparations were made for handling expected adverse weather.

5. Procedures were established for alternate or backup equipment.

Advance preparation was the key to the counter-attack against winter. The early start meant that by mid-October, the airline was ready for anything, including premature snow or freezing rain. So in August, station managers met with airport managers and laid out the snow removal blueprint—all runways must be plowed immediately to a width of at least 100 feet; icy runways must be sanded; on runways plowed less than 125 feet wide, no snowbanks can be higher than three feet; no ridges of snow left at the ends of runways; if snow isn't cleared beyond threshold lights, the edge of the plowed area has to be marked in some way—such as with small Christmas trees (shades of Charlie Cox at Hibbing!); all taxiways, ramps and passenger walkways must be well defined and kept clear. That was Phase One of Operation Cold Front.

Hancock/Houghton Station Manager Nathan Ruonavaara clears snow away from a Convair 440. Under North Central's "Operation Cold Front" program, all stations make advance preparations for severe winter weather.

Forty-one company employees, who were with the airline when operations began, gathered for the Fifteenth Anniversary "Pioneer Dinner" in 1963. Seated are (from left) Milt Ellyson, Bob Gren, George Roycraft, Magnus Budzien, John Downing, Hal Carr, Joe Dick, George Bell, Matt Ruper, Fred Kremer, and Ray Ashley. Standing are (from left) Bob Ceronsky, Gordon Torkelson, Gale Lorsbach, Harold Ebelt, Myron Broten, Art Schwandt, Bob Allison, Jim Grant, Bill Banks, Walt Kneller, Pete Petit, Jack Starry, Tom Needham, Charlie Cox, Pete Hofman, Ralph Parkinson (behind), Frank Seitz (front), Herb Splettstoeser, Ken Schuck, Oscar Malotky, Dick Cooper, Hal Picquet, Art Hinke, Bob Swennes, Joe Sims, Ray Miller (front) Chuck Nason (behind), Lloyd Franke, Don Planck and Ken Sersland. (Not shown are Earl Barron, Joe DeCoursin, and Francis Van Hoof.)

Mountains of snow often confront station personnel and flight crews at most stops on North Central's system. The airline is plagued by such weather for about six months of every year, which is longer than any other airline in the country.

Phase Two, equipment winterization, was accomplished by North Central automotive mechanics or by local garages at the smaller stations. The third stage required that each station keep a wall chart for recording regular inspections and maintenance on all ground support units. Equipment was tested at least twice a day; there was no excuse for anything like a battery failure. This phase also included thorough training of employees by technical personnel who visited the fifty stations where aircraft might be kept overnight.

The training manuals, incidentally, reflected not only a desire for efficiency but Carr's hatred of waste; a manual on the use of deicing spray contained this advice:

> "Operate as required for light frost or ice. Play over wings and tail surface and fuselage when necessary. Avoid windows, ports and cutouts. Remember, you are not washing the airplane."

Operation Cold Front also called for North Central to be operating a small-scale version of the United States Weather Bureau. Those old

At the January 1962 annual meeting of the Association of Local Transport Airlines in Washington, D.C. are (from left) Presidents Ed Converse, Bonanza; Keith Kahle, Central; Nick Bez, West Coast; Tom Davis, Piedmont; Les Barnes, Allegheny; Hal Carr, North Central; Gwin Hicks, Lake Central; Jack Connelly, Pacific. In back, M. K. Smith, Cordova; Bob Ellis, Ellis; Joe FitzGerald, Ozark; Bob Peach, Mohawk; Charles Willis, Alaska; Sig Wien, Wien Alaska; Ray Petersen, Northern Consolidated; Frank Hulse, Southern; Bob Reeve, Reeve Aleutian; Ken Char, Aloha; Earl McKaughan, Trans-Texas.

weather reporting duties of the pioneer station managers came in handy, for now they trained others in weather observations. All stations became adept at spotting cold weather trends, often ahead of the Weather Bureau itself. In some towns, North Central actually hired local residents as temporary station employees, men whose long experience helped them accurately predict snow if there wasn't any official precipitation within 100 miles. Bob Baker, who by 1961 had been named Superintendent of Stations (Needham was now Director of Ground Operations), had a large hand in preparing Cold Front and remembers that these local forecasters could almost smell a coming snowstorm.

"I was accused of hiring Eskimos for these jobs," he confided.

Preparation—that was the magic word. Expect the worst and be ready for it—from scheduling adequate manpower to storing up mops, brooms and shovels, should fancy plows or deicing rigs break down. In one case, a station manager contracted to borrow the equipment of a tree-spraying company if an emergency arose—a fine arrangement for the sprayer, whose services were not exactly in great demand during northern Wisconsin winters.

North Central's "Idea Dollars" program continues to reward employees for worthwhile suggestions. Mechanic Glenn Edberg (center), who made the best contribution in 1961, receives a bonus check from Industrial Relations Vice President Arthur Schwandt (left) and Vice President of Maintenance and Engineering R. H. (Rick) Bendio.

Among those enjoying the 1962 employee picnic were (from left) Regional Superintendent of Station Operations Dick Cooper, Director of Ground Operations Tom Needham, President Hal Carr, Manager of Fleet Service George Karnas, and Manager of Cargo Administration John Minerich.

North Central's directors held their first meeting of 1962 in the new Board room at the general office. Seated around the table are, from left, Werner L. Christensen, Wausau, Wisconsin; A. James Mueller, Milwaukee; David E. Crooker, Ontonagon, Michigan; Arthur E. A. Mueller, Wausau, Chairman; Hal N. Carr, President; Kenneth B. Willett, Stevens Point, Wisconsin; A. L. Wheeler, Washington, D. C.; and G. F. DeCoursin, Clintonville, Wisconsin.

The Convairs proved to be good winter airplanes; so were the DC-3s. They had to be, for twenty of North Central's aircraft sat outside at overnight stations where no hangar facilities were available. Temperatures could run so low that tires froze to the ground. If an automobile owner winterized his car the way North Central had to maintain its planes, he would be shelling out several hundred dollars every fall.

North Central's station manager at Hancock/Houghton, Michigan, Nate Ruonavaara, contributed mightily to Cold Front by designing an engine cover that fitted between the engine and propeller. His first models were of plywood, but fiber glass was later used. The cover was simply a circular board with a U-shaped cutout at the bottom. It not only retained engine heat, but slowed down the cooling rate by allowing oil to drain gradually from the cylinders when a plane had to be parked outside overnight.

Engines were preheated at least one hour before scheduled start-up time—which was thirty minutes before scheduled departure. In addition to engine-starting practices, North Central pilots followed other flight procedures geared to winter operation.

Every aspect of Operation Cold Front contributed to "weatherproofing" the airline for winter reliability. This effective program is one of the primary reasons that North Central, despite bad weather over its system much of the time, has achieved—year after year—one of the best schedule completion records in the industry.

Cold Front had been in operation a year when Carr sent a fair-sized North Central delegation southward—considerably southward, and not for any vacation.

156

This was the company's famed mission to Bolivia, probably the most unusual project ever undertaken by a regional airline. In September of 1963, North Central was awarded a two-year contract to provide managerial and technical assistance to Bolivia's national airline, Lloyd Aereo Boliviano (LAB). The remuneration by the U. S. Agency for International Development (AID) was a solid $800,000, and North Central earned every penny. The Wisconsin Central of 1948 was like American, TWA or United, compared to LAB in 1963.

North Central got into the act when AID asked for bids to help out the South American airline. A number of trunklines bid on the contract, but the State Department liked Carr's idea of sending North Central's own

Project Chief Charles L. Gallo (left) greets North Central President Hal Carr and AID Representative Richard H. McMahon as they deplane in Cochabamba, Bolivia. Carr and McMahon made the trip in November 1963 to review the North Central team's progress toward rehabilitation of Lloyd Aereo Boliviano, the national airline. Behind McMahon are LAB President Julio Pantoja and his assistant, Ricardo Bonel. The U.S. Agency for International Development (AID) awarded North Central a two-year contract for the project.

North Central Captain Arthur Hinke (second from left) visits with LAB's Captain Gonzales (left), Captain ReVollo and Flight Attendant Mendoza. Hinke, who helped establish standard procedures for Bolivian flight crews, holds a small parrot (called a "loro") native to the area. The bird would say "come here" in Spanish and "I don't want to" in English.

employees to Bolivia instead of the experts the trunks were proposing to hire. Among Carr's reasons for seeking the Bolivian assignment was his feeling that it would be a tremendous training ground for some of North Central's younger executives.

The only outside expert hired was Charles Gallo, whom Carr worked with in TWA's general office years before. Gallo had later become Vice President of TACA, a Central American airline partially owned by TWA. He was named Project Chief.

Vice President Rick Bendio headed the Maintenance Division, assisted by Line Specialist Gale Lorsbach and Earl Jackson, Aircraft Engine Technician; while Vice President "Nemo" Niemeyer as Safety Specialist and Art Hinke, Flight Technician, were in charge of flying operations. Dave Moran, at the time Buttomer's staff assistant, was the ranking Traffic and Sales official. North Central Accountant Walt Nielsen supervised Finance and Accounting, with Carl Mills, Assistant Purchasing Manager, assigned to procurement. This group stayed in Bolivia during most of the project. Other specialists in the North Central contingent, including Treasurer Dan May, came for periods varying from six to twelve months.

158

Outside the Cochabamba airport terminal in Bolivia, North Central President Hal Carr (left) chats with LAB Project Chief Charles Gallo.

North Central was honored by the Wisconsin Historical Society with a marker at Clintonville, where the company was founded as Wisconsin Central Airlines in 1944. Company and civic officials attending the dedication on June 21, 1964, are (from left) Arthur Schwandt, Vice President-Industrial Relations; Frank Buttomer, Vice President-Traffic and Sales; Donald Olson, Chairman, Wisconsin State Aeronautics Commission; Eugene Dexter, Chairman, Clintonville Airport Commission; Herbert Foth of Foth & Porath, Inc. and one of the first directors of Wisconsin Central; Duane Petit, an early Wisconsin Central pilot; and Mayor Frank Sinkewicz of Clintonville.

159

Bolivia's President Victor Paz Estenssoro (left) meets with (continuing left) North Central President Hal Carr and LAB Project staff members Charles Gallo, Daniel May, Arthur Hinke, David Moran and Carl Mills in La Paz, the capital.

LAB, a venerable airline established in 1925, had gone downhill to the point of near collapse. Its fleet consisted of two DC-6Bs, seven DC-3/C-47s and three B-17 bombers, modified as cargo planes. When the project started, however, only eight of the twelve aircraft were flyable—one DC-6B, five DC-3s and two of the B-17s. The others were being cannibalized for spare parts, and the headquarters at Cochabamba looked like an aeronautical graveyard. Gallo reported to Vice President-Finance Bud Sweet, who was serving as Home Office coordinator for the project, that LAB was in a worse shambles than anyone expected.

No one knew how many passengers were being carried because each passenger on board was being counted everytime the flight stopped at a station. There were no published timetables or tariffs, and no reservations system. Technical manuals were not current, some being as much as eight years back. Many of the pilots were several months overdue for their proficiency checks, and flying techniques were out-of-date. A preliminary look at the books indicated that LAB was losing nearly $100,000 a month—but some of the books were nine months behind!

"One of our biggest problems was selling LAB personnel and officials on our recommendations," Moran relates. "They could find 500 reasons for rejecting a new idea. We used to get more accomplished over a couple of bottles of beer at night than in a five-hour session during working hours—that's when they realized we were only too human, a long way from home and anxious to make friends. One thing we found out quickly was that Bolivians love to play cards, bridge in particular, and some of us learned in a helluva hurry.

"They had too many people—with only eight planes flying, LAB had twice as many employees per airplane as North Central. Nepotism and 'who you knew' were the way of life. We never did solve this completely, but in the end we encouraged officials to put the Airports Division into a corporation separate from LAB and transfer superfluous employees —of which there were an awful lot—to this corporation, subsidized by the Bolivian government."

Hinke tells the flight story vividly:

"LAB's operating problems were massive and their safety record deplorable. At the La Paz Airport, which is 13,400 feet above sea level,

Some of North Central's team members and families wait to greet incoming personnel from the States at the Cochabamba airport. From left are Dusan Yaksic, Dick Cooper, Walt Nielsen, Helen Cooper, Genevieve Gallo, Al Hann, Guillermo Sanabria (LAB), Margaret Hinke, George Roycraft, Irene Hinke, Carl Mills, (hidden) Carol Amundson, Joanne Moran, Rick Bendio, Al Warner, Gordie Amundson. Children are David and Danelle Moran.

Last of LAB's non-operating aircraft is returned to service after overhaul. Shown (left to right) are Gualberto Rodriguez, head of LAB's engine shop; Gale Lorsbach, North Central's Line Maintenance Specialist; Luis Drake, Administrative Assistant; and Bernard Sweet, coordinator of the Bolivian Project and North Central's Vice President-Finance.

they were flying DC-3s. Lose a little power in one engine, and there was but one way to go—down, and rapidly. Cochabamba was the only airport in Bolivia with paved runways when the project started, and the NW-SE strip looked as if it had been worked over by a squadron of bombers. After a year, a concrete runway was finally completed at La Paz (Bolivia's capital).

"LAB was, for all intents and purposes, a regional carrier like North Central. It was operating only two long-haul routes, and the rest were short-haul. The pilots were capable and intelligent, but their techniques were outmoded, and standardization was limited. One of the first things we did was to requalify all captains in engine-out procedures. Then we started check-riding—using a few choice Spanish cuss words for emphasis."

Some of the obstacles encountered were four-legged. The rat population

162

in LAB's hangars was a positive menace to life, health and property. Moran finally bought a snarling ocelot from a youngster and put the oversized cat into a barrel.

"Every night," he told a Bolivian employee, "let the ocelot out of the barrel, and we won't have rats around here very long."

"One question, senor," the Bolivian asked politely. "What do I do with the ocelot in the morning after he's killed the rats?"

"Put him back in the barrel," Moran said.

"No, senor," was the answer. *"You* put him back in the barrel."

Rat poison was tried next, and the rodents thrived on it. Eventually, someone bought a boa constrictor who decimated the rat population in less than a week.

There were some other diversions, such as an occasional revolution. Once during a bridge game, the players heard gunfire. They just slid down in their chairs below window level, and kept on playing.

Bolivia hosted a reception for North Central's team leaders on November 15, 1963 in La Paz. From left are Ricardo Bonel (LAB), R. H. Bendio, David Moran, Charles Gallo, Hal Carr, Julio Pantoja (LAB President), Daniel May, Carl Mills, Arthur Hinke, Earl Jackson and Gale Lorsbach.

163

A contingent of North Central's LAB Project team gathered at the Cochabamba airport. From left are Flight Safety Specialist A. D. Niemeyer, Airline Accounting Specialist Walter Nielsen, AID Chief of Industrial Development (Latin American Division) Richard McMahon, Rate Specialist Al Hann, Project Chief Charles Gallo, North Central President Hal Carr, Captain Rodolfo Galindo (LAB General Operations Manager), Procurement Specialist Carl Mills, Maintenance Technician R. H. Bendio, Line Maintenance Specialist Gale Lorsbach, Aircraft Engine Overhaul Technician Earl Jackson, Flight Operations Technician Captain Arthur Hinke, Flight Dispatch Technician Joseph Sims, and Marketing/Publicity Specialist David Moran. (Not shown are Pilot Training Technician Randall Sohn and Maintenance Planning Technician David Brown.)

When Moran flew into the Potosi Airport, he found that the runway tilted uphill toward the terminal.

"It was the first airplane I was ever in," he recalls, "where you had to put the chocks *behind* the wheels."

The North Central group got along fine with Gallo who was a character, and could easily have had Wisconsin Central blood in his veins. One day he showed up bragging that he had just purchased a large stock of DC-3 parts at a very low price. After a truck went over to pick up the parts, it

Sherm Booen, Twin Cities aviation journalist, celebrates his Tenth Anniversary in 1963 as host of WCCO-TV's "World of Aviation" program. North Central has sponsored the show since 1954.

was discovered that every piece had "LAB" stamped on it. Gallo had bought part of the airline's spares from a nearby fixed-base operator.

Back in the States, the pace at North Central increased as many people took over the jobs normally done by the management and technical personnel involved in the Bolivian project. No replacements were added so the two-year program provided extra responsibility and a training period for both groups.

As team members came and went, the Home Office staff served as a clearing house for transportation arrangements, personal requests, family emergencies, and the constant flow of information and materials. Besides this, comprehensive quarterly progress reports were prepared and submitted—in English and Spanish—to AID in Washington, D.C. and to LAB.

Poor communications between Cochabamba and the Twin Cities plagued the program. Telephoning was next to impossible, and the mail was erratic. A shortwave radio operator helped with personal calls, but could not transmit business messages. When heading for the States or Bolivia, individuals automatically became "couriers"—laden with packages, letters and lists.

Carr made periodic trips to Bolivia, and at one point sent Charlotte Westberg down to garner a firsthand report on developments. The North Central staff lined up a full week's sightseeing only to have Charlotte spend the time visiting with each one, noting suggestions and problems they wanted relayed to Carr. She was no longer just a secretary; she was a corporate official sent to do a job, and in a sense, her own maturity was the airline's, too.

Sweet also came down to help LAB put in modern accounting procedures and streamline administrative functions. LAB was realigned into five departments—flight operations, maintenance and engineering, traffic and sales, finance and accounting, and an airports division—roughly along the same lines as North Central. Before the two years were up, the North Central personnel and their families who served a Bolivian tour of duty totaled about 100 persons.

North Central maintenance people worked well with their more inexperienced Bolivian counterparts. In a relatively short time, they had the second DC-6B back in service so it could be scheduled on long-haul mountainous flights with a third one that LAB acquired, and had all three of the cargo B-17s flying.

One source of LAB's maintenance difficulties was the weird work schedule: 1 p.m. to 8 p.m. This was changed to a more Americanized shift of 8 a.m. to 6 p.m. The Bolivians were surprised and impressed when the North Central technicians worked beside them to demonstrate how to do something. Other groups had been sent to Bolivia before, but none had really rolled up their sleeves and gotten dirty. Training classes were also started and manuals revised.

To improve public relations, an advertising department and budget were established. The entire LAB operation was spruced up—from new machines for propeller overhaul to new uniforms for ticket agents—and facilities were repaired and painted. LAB was prodded into issuing a public timetable, and one that reflected more realistic scheduling. For example, LAB had a route segment with heavy traffic but few flights,

Ted Cole, member of the Wisconsin State Aeronautics Commission and a North Central Presidential Advisor, tours the airline's general office and main operations base with President Hal Carr in 1964.

while another had light traffic and many flights. Interestingly enough, weather was a prime scheduling factor—LAB put less flights on the route with weather problems. Needless to say, weather-conscious North Central changed this pattern of thinking in a hurry. Aircraft availability also limited the scope of scheduling. As more planes were returned to flying status, flights could be added and utilization increased.

Given an effective operating blueprint, there was no reason for LAB to continue what had been six successive years of substantial losses. The airline's load factors were unusually high for both passengers and cargo—a healthy 70-80 percent. The market was there; the Bolivians simply needed modern technical and promotional know-how to tap it, and North Central provided this assistance. Before the Americans left, LAB was not only flying its Bolivian routes more efficiently and safely, but had inaugurated a new Bolivia-Brazil route that was carrying near-capacity loads.

Among other accomplishments, North Central's advisors produced a South American version of "Herman".

"It was a stylized Bolivian condor in flight," Moran reminisces, "and is still being used."

Several events affected the overall rehabilitation program for LAB. Bolivia itself changed presidents, and there were three presidents of the airline during the two-year period. But the LAB personnel seemed to take this in stride, and progress continued.

One of the North Central group's final tasks was an aircraft evaluation study; it was obvious that LAB's fleet was obsolete and newer planes were needed. Turbine equipment was essential because much of LAB's high operating costs was due to the 65¢-to-$1 a gallon the Bolivian carrier was paying for high octane gasoline that had to be imported. In contrast, jet fuel could be produced locally in any quantity and at competitive U. S. prices.

The study proposed two alternatives, and either could have changed the red ink to black. The first, promising the most dramatic short-range improvement, recommended the purchase of a Lockheed Electra II for international routes and two Convair 580 prop-jets for primary domestic use. (The study named the Boeing 727 as the best aircraft on LAB's international routes, but it was not seriously considered because of the high price tag and relative unavailability.)

The other alternative still advocated the Electra II internationally, but favored Fokker F-27s for domestic flights—provided all DC-3s were replaced. Actually, the team preferred the Hawker Siddeley 748 which had superior characteristics over the Fokker at sub-standard airports, but felt AID wouldn't hold still for buying British aircraft.

It is interesting to note that several years later LAB followed the recommendations and acquired an Electra, two F-27s and eventually, a 727. These aircraft proved to be very efficient and productive in the airline's operation.

The North Central advisors departed from Bolivia with Lloyd Aereo Boliviano well on its way to a happier future. Many suggestions weren't put into effect until the Americans were back home—Bolivian pride seemed to have delayed their acceptance temporarily. But North Central had done a superb job, and Hal Carr gained far more than the $800,000 fee—he had trained a large chunk of his younger management team to run an airline from scratch.

And more important, the project in many ways was a dress rehearsal for what Carr knew was coming inevitably:

Herman was heading for the jet age.

The familiar "Hermans" appear in formation on the tails of Convair 440 Northliners parked at Chicago O'Hare International Airport. This picture appeared on the cover of "Flight Magazine" when the Fifteenth Annual Local Air Service edition was printed in 1964.

CHAPTER SEVEN

Jet Power

North Central was now ready to acquire jet aircraft, but the analysis that went into the decision mirrored Carr's inherent cautiousness toward commitments fraught with peril if the wrong airplane were purchased. He could study the industry and see many examples of such folly.

Carr had three choices: the British BAC-111, the Douglas DC-9 and Boeing's 737. A North Central aircraft evaluation committee rejected the BAC-111 because it was too small. The 737 was ranked high, but by the time North Central decided to buy jets, the Boeing entry had been victimized by the third-pilot controversy—it was now official ALPA policy to require a three-man crew for the twin-engine 737, an aircraft specifically designed for a two-man crew. And Carr wasn't taking any chances that North Central's pilots, however loyal, would buck ALPA policy.

The choice boiled down to the DC-9, but Carr wasn't entirely satisfied with the early model, known as the DC-9 Series 10. The evaluation group agreed with him that the plane was the most suitable, but a bit small. Carr held off the final selection, and by waiting he got a fourth choice—and a far better one: Douglas began building a larger version of the DC-9, the DC-9—30 series, which had twenty-five more seats than the Series 10 and cost only a little more. This was the plane Carr wanted, and he assigned Bud Sweet, Vice President-Finance, to the task of raising the enormous sum needed for the purchase.

In July of 1965, North Central took the plunge. It ordered five 100-passenger DC-9s for $20 million and took an option on five more. Sweet, working with Treasurer Dan May, arranged for a $17-million line of credit with the Irving Trust and the Northwestern National Bank, along with some of its affiliates, at the extremely favorable interest rate of 5¼ percent. There wasn't any question but that the interest rate was kept low

Signing the agreement in July 1965 for North Central's initial ten-jet program is President Hal Carr. Also participating are John Burton, left, Regional Sales Manager for Douglas Aircraft and Bernard Sweet, North Central's Vice President-Finance.

because of the airline's strong financial position—North Central netted more than $1.1 million in 1965 on record revenues of $33.9 million.

Under the original purchase agreement, Douglas was to deliver three jets in 1967 and two more in 1968. Meanwhile, North Central beefed up its piston-engine fleet with six more Convair 440s, bringing the Convair total to thirty, while some of the remaining sixteen DC-3s were being used as all-cargo aircraft.

Art Mueller never lived to counsel Carr on the airline's greatest aircraft investment move. On March 15, 1965, North Central's Chairman of the Board died suddenly, and Carr grieved the loss of an old and treasured friend.

Board Chairman Arthur Mueller (white coat) meets with dignitaries in Oshkosh. At right is North Central Vice President R. H. (Rick) Bendio.

"He was all man," Carr says fondly. "A big, husky, outgoing guy who never interfered. If I had told him I was going to sell the airplanes and buy buses, he would have said okay, go ahead; it's your show."

Mueller was wealthy, a Phi Beta Kappa, and the holder of two college degrees, including a Master's from Cornell, but he was also as informal and casual as a sailor on shore leave. When he visited North Central's general office, employees could spot him coming a block away. His favorite costume consisted of purple slacks, a loud sport jacket, blue suede shoes, argyle socks and a white leather trench coat he had won in a poker game.

His sartorial taste drove Carr up the wall. They were visiting England for talks with the British Aircraft Corporation on the BAC-111, and through an entire conference Mueller kept staring at a BAC official equipped with a bowler hat and an umbrella. The next day, Mueller bought a similar outfit, and for the rest of the trip kept telling everyone he was Carr's "man servant."

"Some man servant," Carr growled affectionately. "He looked like the poor man's Sebastian Cabot."

He showed up in Carr's office one day full of chortling enthusiasm.

"I've just gotten some great publicity for North Central," he boasted.

It turned out he had won a lot of money at the races, and as he was leaving the track, after toasting his winnings, he spotted a young black boy extremely skilled at the one-man band act. Mueller paid the youngster $10 to play "When the Saints Come Marching In" and supplied slightly altered vocals. The revisions consisted of a new opening line: "I'm Chairman of the Board of North Central Airlines."

"That's just great," Carr said. "But where's the publicity for the airline?"

"Hell, chum," Mueller beamed, "I must have had a thousand people watching me."

"I'll just bet you did," Carr said, shaking his head.

A few days after Mueller's death, the Board met and named Carr Chairman, in addition to his positions as President and General Manager. It was only one of several major title changes that year—Tom Needham was promoted to Vice President-Ground Operations, Red Wallis to Vice President-Flight Operations, and Keely replaced the retiring Bendio as Vice President-Maintenance and Engineering.

Another North Central veteran retired, too—sort of. One of the DC-3s purchased from Eastern in 1952, old "728", made its final scheduled trip on April 26, 1965. It left Milwaukee at 6:25 a.m. as Flight 2 with Captain Jim Robb and First Officer Jay Thomas at the controls, arriving Chicago at 7 a.m.

The venerable DC-3 took off again at 7:30 a.m. as Flight 467, back to Milwaukee, then on to Madison, LaCrosse and the Twin Cities, landing at 10:59 a.m. After servicing and cleaning, 728 left at 3:30 p.m., this time as Flight 757, for Brookings, Huron and Pierre, South Dakota. A new crew had boarded in Minneapolis/St. Paul, and fittingly, the captain for the final legs was veteran Herb Splettstoeser—it was one of the last trips he was to make before retirement. The first officer was Jim Topping.

The return flight to the Twin Cities was 758. By the end of the day, the DC-3 had carried 111 passengers and—true to form—it had flown every segment on time. As of the moment its wheels touched down at the Minneapolis-St. Paul International Airport (10:19 p.m.), 728 had logged 83,032 hours, 52 minutes of flying time since the date of its manufacture. It had traveled over twelve million miles, or the equivalent of twenty-five trips to the moon and back.

In compiling that incredible record, 728 also produced more than 260 million passenger miles. Translated into simpler statistics, that would be the same as taking the entire population of Chicago for a thirty-minute hop, twenty-one passengers at a time, or flying everyone in Dallas to Oklahoma City and back. The plane, during its lifetime with Eastern and North Central, wore out 550 main gear tires, 25,000 spark plugs and 136

Admiring a one-tenth scale model of the DC-9 jet are (from left) Vice President-Ground Operations Tom Needham; Vice President-Industrial Relations Arthur Schwandt; Vice President-Maintenance and Engineering Les Keely; and Vice President-Finance Bernard Sweet. The model was on display at the North Central station managers' meeting in October 1965.

North Central's DC-3 bearing serial number N21728 was retired from service on April 26, 1965, having logged 83,032 hours and 52 minutes—more time in the air than any other aircraft in the history of aviation. The plane was completely remodeled for its new promotional duties, and a picture window was added on each side, but 90 percent of the airframe is just as it was when "728" rolled off the Douglas assembly line in 1939.

Donald W. Douglas, Sr. (left), Chairman of the Board, Douglas Aircraft Company, presents North Central President Hal N. Carr with a bronze plaque (photo below) citing "728" as the World's High-Time Aircraft.

The plush new interior of "728" features walnut paneling, deluxe chairs and divan, a television, AM radio and stereo. Maintenance personnel are shown in the aircraft. From left, Harold Ebelt, Manager-Quality Control; Jack Starry, Superintendent-Base Overhaul; seated, (left) Gerald DeGrand, Systems Service Engineer; and John Fager, Production Planning Statistician.

Taking a break at La Guardia Airport in New York, after filming a DC-3 documentary featuring North Central's "728", are (from left) Captain Julian Carr, Jr.; Manager-Flight Crews Arthur Hinke; entertainer Arthur Godfrey; Assistant Stewardess Training Supervisor Carol Shanahan; President Hal Carr; and Manager-Public Relations Richard Woodbury. Godfrey narrated the film which was produced by WZZM-TV (Grand Rapids, Michigan).

engines. It burned eight million gallons of gasoline which would be enough to run an automobile for about 11,000 years. Someone even figured out that 728 had taxied well over 100,000 miles.

Carr refused to let the old bird retire. He ordered 728 refitted into what amounted to a combination corporate airplane and flying laboratory. It was among the first North Central planes to be equipped with Distance Measuring Equipment (DME). Its cabin was used to test various accessories and color schemes. But most important, 728 became an affectionate, nostalgic symbol of the past. Its rather spartan cabin was refitted into one of the most luxurious DC-3 interiors ever designed. Seating capacity was reduced from twenty-six to eleven. Appointments include blue wool carpeting specially created in Puerto Rico, a down-filled divan, a large galley and bar, lounge-type lavatory, and indirect lighting. Cabin wall linings were stripped out and replaced by lightweight walnut with a contrasting band of bamboo matting which blended nicely with the beige ceiling. Three tables, table lamps, a television set, AM radio, and stereo tape player completed 728's metamorphosis.

North Central Chairman and President Hal Carr and guests of the airline prepare to board "728". From left are Eric Bramley, Vice President of American Aviation Publications, Washington, D. C.; Dr. Malcolm Moos, University of Minnesota President; Carr; Mrs. Morton Phillips ("Dear Abby"); Morton Phillips, North Central director; Dr. Orly Foster, Minneapolis; and Paul Willson, President of Gay Gibson, Inc., Kansas City.

Carr was fascinated with the face-lifting job and still uses 728 as often as possible, although it must be admitted that North Central's mechanics don't quite share his unrequited affection. DC-3 spare parts are hard to get, and DC-3 engines somewhat difficult to maintain for men acclimated to the turbines. But it's possible that 728 will keep flying in North Central's colors as long as parts are available; the aircraft is an intriguing public relations vehicle used frequently for transporting VIPs, civic officials and press representatives. A visitor's first look at the swank interior produces almost the same awe as an initial introduction to a 747.

Everything was going well for North Central. However, Carr was increasingly concerned about what was fast becoming a serious problem: the slowdown in route development. It wasn't from lack of effort. In 1965, North Central was involved in seven major route cases, but the wheels of the Civil Aeronautics Board ground slowly. The truth was that the airline's growth in terms of route expansion had come to a virtual halt. Not since 1960, when the Great Lakes decision was announced, had the company received a really lucrative route. The majority of the awards were short-haul. Even as North Central began ordering jets, its average hop was only 88 miles, and the average passenger flew only 169 miles. All Carr could do was get ready for what had to be done if better routes were forthcoming.

One thing he set in motion for the future was the construction of a new $17-million general office and main operations base to be built at the Minneapolis-St. Paul International Airport. In the Spring of 1965, when North Central was still an all-piston airline, Carr called in John P. Dow,

Minneapolis/St. Paul Mechanic Harlan Renstrom (left) shows Manager-Base Overhaul George Roycraft a new way to repair the bottom cowlings on Convair aircraft. Renstrom, who received $100 for the suggestion in 1966, had already won four other cash awards through the company's "Idea Dollars" program.

176

corporate Secretary. Dow was an ex-fighter pilot who was about to join a Minneapolis advertising firm after the Korean War when he heard there was a job open at North Central as Properties Manager. He grabbed it and rose rapidly.

"One of these days," Carr told him, "we're gonna be getting jet equipment. We have to know how to maintain it and where to put it. As I see it, we've got two choices: we either expand our present facilities or we build a brand-new base, and if it's the latter, where the hell do we put it? I need some answers, Jack."

"How soon?" Dow asked.

"The Board meets in July. I want a tentative plan by then, including a layout for a new general office and all the hangar space we can get."

Before the July deadline, Dow met almost daily with consultants and engineering firms. He finally selected Quinton Engineers to do a feasibility study of all alternatives, to wit: expansion of present facilities versus a new site. Quinton recommended a new location, pointing out that expansion was virtually impossible because of lack of land.

Three sites were considered. The best was a 102-acre plot south of the airport, being farmed under a lease arrangement. North Central convinced the Minneapolis-St. Paul Metropolitan Airports Commission to make the land available to the airline.

The site had two chief advantages. For one thing, it was big enough to allow for almost unlimited future expansion. Second, the proposed area

North Central's main base in the Twin Cities was suitable for the Convairs and DC-3s, but not adequate for jet operations. Management offices rimmed the upper perimeter of the hangars.

On December 18, 1965, North Central sold the first DC-3 it had purchased from Trans World Airlines in January 1951. The aircraft, N17320, had rolled off the Douglas Aircraft assembly line in December 1940. When sold, the plane had flown 78,267 hours and 44 minutes; nearly 34,000 of these hours were logged during the fourteen years the DC-3 was flying the "Route of the Northliners".

was on the fringe of Interstate 494, a heavily traveled superhighway. There was plenty of exposure to the public, which still might have had reason for wondering if there really was a North Central.

The plans called for a hangar 750 feet long, a structure plainly visible from Highway 494, so Dow okayed the purchase of a gigantic sign with the letters NORTH CENTRAL AIRLINES running the entire length of the building, and neon lighting at night. The sign alone cost $50,000 (it was the biggest one in the state), but Carr regarded it as inexpensive advertising.

The land lease agreement was for 102 acres over a thirty-year period. It wasn't consummated until the summer of 1966, after Carr had invited the Airports Commission to a small dinner and reviewed the plan for the headquarters complex. Meanwhile, he had other problems to solve that dwarfed the building of a new main base.

Serious complications arose after Mueller's death in the liquidation of his estate. Mueller's largest asset was 55 percent of North Central's stock, and it was obvious that the best way his family could pay the inheritance taxes and settle the estate was to sell the stock. Carr knew that dumping some five million shares of the company's 8.7 million outstanding shares might allow outsiders to seize control of North Central. Several corporations and wealthy individuals were interested in purchasing the entire Mueller block of stock, but Carr acted fast enough to stall any stock sale—for, in effect, the airline itself was suddenly up for sale.

Finally, North Central Director Joseph E. Rapkin, an executor and attorney for the Mueller estate, worked with Ferdinand Eberstadt, head of F. Eberstadt & Co., New York investment bankers, to develop a plan for a secondary stock offering. Briefly, the plan called for selling five million shares of the Mueller stock by offering 2.5 million North

Central Airlines "units", each unit consisting of one share of stock and one warrant to purchase a second share at $3.25 by the fall of 1968. The price per unit was $3, and the sale of the 2.5 million units brought $7.5 million in cash to the estate, less discounts and commissions.

The other 2.5 million shares were held in escrow to meet the warrant purchases. Carr and a group of Minneapolis investors then agreed to buy the 2.5 million escrow shares at a discount price of $2.75 a share, subject to the prior rights of the warrant holders, so the estate could be closed. In October 1968, the market price of the stock was around $6.50, and those holding the warrants to buy stock at $3.25 snapped up most of the 2.5 million shares in escrow before the warrants expired on November 1.

Today, North Central's over twelve million outstanding shares are spread among nearly 40,000 owners. Although Carr is the largest individual stockholder, no owner has more than five percent, and the average holding per stockholder is about 300 shares. North Central's situation is in marked contrast to the many airlines that are controlled by large companies outside the aviation industry.

The CAB's delay in approving North Central's route applications was particularly serious with the DC-9s coming up, literally an airplane that was too big and too fast for most of the route structure. Yet there was no choice; with a two-year lead time between order and delivery, Carr had to gamble on some long-range awards coming through by the time the new jets were scheduled to go into operation. There was one more factor to consider:

Vice President Hubert H. Humphrey is welcomed by Jon Harty, North Central's Staff Assistant to the Vice President-Traffic and Sales, after completing a 1966 campaign tour to several Minnesota cities on a North Central charter.

from every iota of evidence on hand, turbine-powered equipment was far cheaper to operate than pistons. Carr put down his bets.

In August of 1966, he exercised North Central's option on the second batch of five DC-9s, with a 1968 delivery. The schedule remained at three in 1967 and increased to seven in 1968 (instead of two). This required more negotiations with the banks—Sweet and May began discussions on raising the $17-million line of credit to $35 million. They were a little premature—and somewhat inadequate. For at the same time, North Central announced it was converting two-thirds of its Convair fleet (twenty out of thirty-one aircraft) to the Allison-powered turboprop known as the Convair 580, with an option for converting the other eleven.

It was obvious that the substantial amount of money needed to complete this re-equipment program would exceed the lending capacities of the two banks which had financed the first DC-9s.

The problem was discussed with several lenders and investment bankers. After reviewing the cost of having an investment firm find the additional money, it was decided the financing package could be put

Businessmen, servicemen, and vacationers formed long lines from morning to evening at North Central's ticket counters. Encouraged by the demand for seats and possible new route awards, North Central accelerated its schedule for delivery of the DC-9 jets.

Late in 1966, construction was completed on the new maintenance facility at Detroit Metropolitan Airport.

together by having Sweet and May make their own contacts and save the placement fee of around $500,000.

This started a lengthy search for long-term lenders. The first big hurdle was cleared when Aetna Life Insurance Company and The Connecticut General Life Insurance Company agreed to take $10 million and $5 million. While in Hartford one day to visit these companies, Sweet and May drove by the Connecticut Mutual Life Insurance Building. Sweet suggested they stop and see if the firm might have an interest in participating in the loan. The unplanned visit eventually resulted in a $2-million commitment.

Another organization which played an important role in the financing was The Northwestern Mutual Life Insurance Company of Milwaukee. This company, noted for its conservative investments, was contacted several times. Finally, after a number of meetings, Northwestern Mutual committed to $5 million. The search for funds continued into 1967.

North Central ended 1966 with another profit of over $1 million, record revenues of just under $40 million, and the loss of a key officer. On November 24, Frank Buttomer died at the age of 62. Carr had been talking with him about retiring. The big guy had a bad heart and high blood pressure—the twin badges of an executive who had been working too hard for too long.

"I'll take it a little easier," Buttomer promised Carr, "but I gotta stay in harness long enough to see us flying jets."

He was so adamant that Carr relented. On November 22, Buttomer suffered a stroke in the middle of the night and was rushed to a hospital where he died two days later. He is still remembered around North Central with affection and respect. And when it came to choosing a successor to the capable, warm-hearted Vice President, Carr picked the man Buttomer himself had once spotted as a comer and had personally trained. It was Dave Moran.

Carr lost Niemeyer that year, too. "Nemo," as everyone called him, had reached retirement age and called it quits after a lifetime in aviation. His departure, plus the deaths of two close friends in less than two years, led Carr into some serious thinking. Working long hours and loading virtually all the responsibilities of the airline on his own shoulders inevitably would take its toll. He wanted a right-hand man, someone he could trust, someone who could run North Central's day-to-day operation while he concentrated on long-range policy matters.

He didn't have to look very far. For some time, he had been watching the performance of quiet, efficient Bud Sweet. Nearly three years younger than Carr, Sweet had demonstrated tremendous capability in every task assigned to him. Carr now named him Executive Vice President and also boosted Dow and May to Vice Presidencies. His management team for the jet age was set, a perfect blending of experienced maturity and aggressive

Glenn L. Humphrey (second from right), President of Humphrey Enterprises, Milwaukee, shows his North Central Presidential Advisor citation to (from left) Director Joseph E. Rapkin; Vice President-Traffic and Sales Frank Buttomer; and Vice President-Ground Operations Tom Needham. Humphrey was named a Presidential Advisor on June 29, 1966.

182

On April 1, 1967, North Central entered the jet age when two Convair 580 Allison-powered prop-jets were placed in scheduled service. The pressurized aircraft carries 48 passengers.

youth. Sweet, Dow, May, Moran and Wallis were the younger corps; Keely, Needham and Schwandt, the elder statesmen.

North Central officially entered the jet age April 1, 1967, with the first two 580 prop-jets going into service and six more joining the fleet before the end of the year. It wasn't exactly a dramatic entrance calling for trumpets and glowing adjectives; some of the other regionals had been operating turbine equipment for as long as two years. The trunklines, of course, had introduced pure jets in 1958.

But Carr was not unhappy with his timing. He had held off on the DC-9 until a better version was available. He had delayed buying the 580 until it had been thoroughly proved on other local service routes. And the new Convair prop-jets turned out to be even better than North Central had

North Central Stewardesses Jill Kilgore (left) and Betty Schmelz presented a silver shovel to President Hal Carr at the ground-breaking ceremony on July 19, 1967, for the airline's new headquarters facility at the Minneapolis-St. Paul International Airport. At right is Vice President R. H. (Rick) Bendio; Secretary and Manager of Properties John Dow is behind the drawing of the general office and main operations base complex.

hoped. Originally, the airline came close to buying a 440 conversion with Rolls-Royce engines instead of Allisons. The British-powered version was called the Convair 640. Maintenance favored the 640 because of the British engine's reputation for reliability, but Flight Operations preferred the more powerful Allison, and Carr went along with this recommendation—a wise choice, it developed, because the 640 eventually had to operate under severe restrictions that reduced its usefulness.

The Convair 580's costs were estimated to be about 15 cents a plane-mile under the 440's. During the first three months of 1967, they actually ran 31 cents less than the pistons. They were so operationally efficient and popular with passengers that Carr decided to go almost whole-hog: convert another six 440s into prop-jets. North Central had thirty-one 440s at the start of 1967; Carr's decision called for conversion of twenty-six of them, which meant that additional financing was necessary.

With Sweet involved in the daily operation of the company, Dan May had to go back to the banks for more money. May, a big, happy-appearing former pastor who belied the impression that career accountants generally resemble dyspeptic undertakers, went to work and completed the financing package. The result was a $62-million loan program. It involved the sale of

North Central's first jet-age "Crew of the Year" received awards from President Hal Carr for 1967. From left are First Officer Bill Hunchis, Stewardess Nancy Squire, Captain Ed Sorensen, Stewardess Martha Haning, First Officer Lyle Palmateer, Captain Bob Chirhart, Stewardess Fran Seidler, First Officer Al Davis and Captain F. (Sandy) Sandeberg.

North Central's Convair 580 prop-jets were popular with passengers and performed so efficiently that the conversion program was expanded.

Vice President of Flight Operations G. F. (Red) Wallis, left, and Manager of Flight Training Peter Wahl run through the DC-9 check list with Captain Robert J. Stone, TWA flight instructor. (Wallis and Wahl made the acceptance flights in California before bringing North Central's first DC-9 to the Twin Cities in 1967. They were to accept and deliver fifteen more by the end of 1972.)

North Central DC-9s dominate the Douglas Aircraft Company assembly line at Santa Monica, California, early in 1967. The airline had ten of the 100-passenger jets on order.

Acceptance ceremonies were held July 22, 1967, in Long Beach, California, prior to the flight of North Central's first DC-9 fan jet to Minneapolis/St. Paul. Vice President-Flight Operations G. F. Wallis (second from right) receives a gold key to the jet from Gerald B. Thomas, Douglas Aircraft Vice President-Domestic Commercial Sales. From left are Stewardess Training Supervisor Mary King; Vice President R. H. Bendio; Corporate Secretary John P. Dow; Thomas; Wallis and Training Supervisor Patricia Manly.

An enthusiastic crowd of North Central personnel (above) welcomes the company's first DC-9 fan jet on arrival in the Twin Cities July 28, 1967. Among those on hand to greet the crew (left photo) was President Hal Carr (right). From left are G. F. (Red) Wallis, Mary King, Peter Wahl and Patricia Manly.

notes to the First National City Bank of New York, Northwestern National Bank of Minneapolis and several of its affiliates, plus a number of insurance companies, as well as some refunding of the existing debt.

Once more, North Central's healthy financial state won attractive interest rates with no equity financing required. The $62 million didn't cover all the costs of the DC-9 purchases and Convair conversions, but the company's cash flow during 1967, which includes funds from depreciation and deferred taxes, was sufficient to pour nearly $5.4 million into the equipment program.

The cash flow stemmed largely from a record $43 million in revenues. Net profits set another record—more than $1.5 million. And the Civil Aeronautics Board finally produced some major route awards—nonstop authority between Detroit and Toronto and North Central's first entry into

Company directors were the first to inspect the new DC-9 fan jet. From left are Chan Gurney, Morton B. Phillips, Samuel H. Maslon, Joseph E. Rapkin, Robert G. Zeller, Hal N. Carr, Kenneth B. Willett, G. F. DeCoursin, A. James Mueller, H. P. Skoglund, and D. E. Crooker.

Service with Douglas DC-9 Series-30 fan jets was inaugurated by North Central on September 8, 1967. The new jet cruises at 560 miles per hour and carries 100 passengers.

Missouri with a nonstop route between Sioux Falls, South Dakota, and Kansas City. Another plum fell into the airline's lap when the CAB picked North Central to replace Braniff at Sioux City and Sioux Falls—which gave Carr a chance to inaugurate new nonstop trips between Sioux Falls and the Twin Cities. The system now added up to ninety cities in eleven states and Canada, a 7,000-mile network that slowly but surely was shaping up as one that could support jet operations.

DC-9 service was inaugurated on September 8, 1967. This was only 160 days after the introduction of the 580s, and probably no other airline had ever put two different types of new aircraft into service in that short a span of time. Preparations for the 580 had been extensive, but they were even more complex for the pure jets. Not long after the DC-9 purchase was

DC-9 promotional flights attracted large numbers of people. The spacious jet cabin features two-and-three-abreast seating with single class service. The stewardess is Judith Davies.

announced, lead mechanics, foremen and supervisors went through a four-week training program at the Douglas plant, while other key maintenance personnel headed for similar schools at Pratt & Whitney and AiResearch. Red Wallis and the Manager of Flight Training, Pete Wahl, were sent through TWA's DC-9 transition program in Kansas City.

Bob Gren, now Keely's Manager of Line Maintenance, was put in charge of determining DC-9 spare parts needs. It was an eye-opener for him. In his own words:

"We were getting around $20,000 apiece for the DC-3s being phased out. I found we had to pay more than that—some $22,000—just for DC-9 cockpit windshield spares. A DC-3 engine cost us only $2,500, and the one for the 340 was $25,000. The price tag for the DC-9 turbine engine was $250,000. I thought it was rough when a 340 engine cost ten times more than the DC-3, but then we wound up paying another ten times more with the new jets."

The old Carr rule of "sometimes-you-gotta-spend-money-to-make-money" was invoked again when it came to DC-9 pilot training. North Central shelled out $75,000 for a new Gemco cockpit procedures trainer, but this saved the airline nearly four flight hours per pilot when they transitioned to the jets. About one month was spent training pilots and ground personnel between July 28, when the first DC-9 taxied up to the hangar ramp at Minneapolis/St. Paul, and the start of scheduled jet service on September 8.

Both the 580s and the DC-9s sported North Central's jet "New Look"—another Brocken creation. He had designated the corporate colors of aqua, dark blue and gold and skillfully blended them into one of the most

Joseph S. Murphy, Editor and Publisher of "Air Transport World," accepts a model of North Central's new DC-9 Series-30 fan jet from Hal Carr, President. Murphy was in the Twin Cities to compile information on North Central for a September 1967 cover story in his publication.

189

*Detroit-Toronto nonstop service was inaugurated August 1, 1967.
Civic leaders from the two cities, press representatives and North
Central personnel took part in the festivities. In the group are Vice
Presidents Dave Moran, Tom Needham and Rick Bendio;
Stewardesses Rita Molland, Shirley Wissman, and Carole Syverson;
District Sales Managers Bill Domres and Bob Shook; and Public
Relations Manager Dick Woodbury.*

*Directors of the airline greet Kansas City business and civic leaders
attending a reception marking the start of Kansas City-Sioux City
nonstop service on December 1, 1967. Directors are (from left) G. F.
DeCoursin, Jay Phillips, Chan Gurney and Chairman Hal Carr.*

190

beautiful designs ever used on an airliner. Herman was present, of course—a deep blue silhouette on the tail bisecting a golden ring—while a wide aqua stripe, the length of the fuselage, accented the white top of the plane. The color combination wasn't really new; Brocken had used aqua, blue and gold on North Central aircraft interiors in 1958 and decided to go with them in an exterior scheme when the jets arrived.

The jets brought an entirely different environment to North Central's family, now over 2,600 employees and two million annual passengers (the 1967 passenger total was 2,347,371). The Flight Control Department was just one example and an illustrative one. Veterans like Joe Sims, Myron Broten and Hal Picquet had started out in the days when "the paperwork always got there before the airplane," as Sims puts it. In 1948, the whole flight control operation involved about a dozen flights a day, with one dispatcher working five or six during his shift. By the time the jet age arrived, a dispatcher was handling as many as twenty flights. The workload became more concentrated, too; with jet schedules, two-thirds of North Central's flights operated in an eight-hour daytime period, with the rest spread over the remaining sixteen hours.

Carr's natural reaction to jet introduction was to continue pouring route applications into Washington as fast as they could be drawn up. By the end of 1967, North Central had filed various route proposals that would have added nearly 10,000 miles to the system, thirteen new cities, six more states and another Canadian province. But the ones he wanted most of all involved two long-haul routes: Milwaukee-New York and Twin Cities-Denver. Both segments were subjects of CAB investigations into adequacy of current service in those areas. The route expansion plan also called for putting North Central into Washington/Baltimore, Philadelphia and Boston via nonstop flights from the Twin Cities or Milwaukee.

Captain Eddie Rickenbacker (left), famed World War I flying ace and long-time head of Eastern Air Lines, appeared on Sherm Booen's "World of Aviation" show in 1968, along with North Central's Manager-Flight Crews Art Hinke, one of the original captains who started with the company in 1948.

It was Happy Birthday to Herman again on February 24, 1968. North Central's Twentieth Anniversary found the company with a fifty-two aircraft fleet, a route system that stretched 7,000 miles, and more passengers every two days than Wisconsin Central had carried during its entire first year. The airline celebrated the occasion by staging a five-plane "Twentieth Anniversary Flight" for photographers. The battered hulk of one of its original Lockheed 10As had been restored to flying condition by Lead Mechanic Lee Koepke of Detroit. The old Electra paced the formation, followed by the DC-3 "728", with a Convair 440 and a 580 next in line, and the new DC-9 last. Aircraft 728 also got into television by playing a leading role in a documentary film on the DC-3, "The Plane That Refused to Die," with Arthur Godfrey doing the narration.

But the proudest achievement of all on the Twentieth Anniversary was in safety: 16.4 million passengers flown 2.7 billion passenger miles without a single fatality or injury to passengers or crew members. North Central had maintained a perfect safety record since the start of service in 1948. Never before had any airline operated so long without a fatal accident.

Employees who were with the airline when scheduled operations began twenty years ago were honored at a "Pioneer Banquet" in Minneapolis/St. Paul on February 28, 1968. Seated are: M. (Bud) Budzien, Pete Hofman, Karl Brocken, G. F. (Joe) DeCoursin, Francis Higgins, Hal Carr, Ray Ashley, Earl Barron, Ralph Parkinson, George Bell, Art Schwandt, and Ken Sersland. Standing, left to right, Frank Seitz, Hal Picquet, Ray Miller, Dick Cooper, Bob Allison, Ken Schuck, Art Hinke, Walt Kneller, Bob Swennes, Bob Gren, A. M. (Bill) Banks, Matt Ruper, Tom Needham, Gale Lorsbach, Charlie Cox, Duane (Pete) Petit, Bob Ceronsky, Oscar Malotky, Chuck Nason, Joe Dick, Francis VanHoof, Jack Starry, John Downing, Myron Broten, George Roycraft, Joe Sims, Milt Ellyson, Don Planck, Lloyd Franke, and Harold Ebelt. (Not shown are Gordon Torkelson and Jim Grant.)

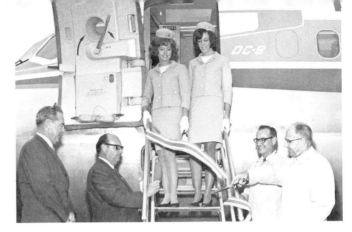

Rochester, Minnesota, was added to North Central's system in 1968 as the intermediate stop on the new Chicago-Sioux Falls, South Dakota, route. Participating in inaugural ceremonies are (from left) J. P. Dunne, First Deputy Commissioner of Aviation, Chicago; North Central Presidential Advisor Joe Floyd, President of Midcontinent Broadcasting Company, Sioux Falls; Stewardesses Cheryl Maddox and Sue Achbach; Architect John Brengman, President of the Rochester Chamber of Commerce; and Mayor Michael Schirmer of Sioux Falls.

Route development continued on the slow side. The only new service inaugurated in 1968 was the addition of Rochester, Minnesota, on the Chicago-Sioux Falls route and the introduction of nonstop service between the Twin Cities and Milwaukee, and Milwaukee-Detroit.

The CAB did agree to let North Central consolidate its sixteen-segment system into five, eliminating certain operating restrictions—it was a realignment that permitted longer flights, greater scheduling flexibility and better fleet utilization. The Board also established shortened hearing procedures aimed at faster action on petitions for nonstop service on existing routes. The Twin Cities-Milwaukee and Milwaukee-Detroit nonstops were North Central's first applications approved under the streamlined operation.

But no less than sixteen other route proposals were still somewhere on the CAB assembly line in various stages of incompletion. Because of the heavy expenditures involved in the jet transition, net profits fell to only $70,000 despite a new high in revenues—$55.2 million. At that, North Central was lucky to stay out of the red; not only did operating expenses rise 27 percent from the 1967 level, but interest payments on the equipment loans totalled over $3 million.

On December 3, 1968, North Central's Public Relations Manager, Delmar Drumm, typed out a proud news release. It reported that on December 1, the airline had set a new record of daily passenger boardings, carrying 12,666 on that one day. Drumm noted that the total was 1,268 more than the 11,398 passengers who flew Wisconsin Central during its first year of operation.

193

Hal N. Carr, North Central Chairman of the Board and President, gave other directors a progress tour, in September 1968, of the construction site for the airline's new general office and main operations base located at the Twin Cities International Airport. Board members present include (from left) D. E. Crooker, Joseph E. Rapkin, Carr, Jay Phillips, Samuel H. Maslon, G. F. DeCoursin, Kenneth B. Willett, Morton B. Phillips, H. P. Skoglund, and Chan Gurney. (Not pictured are Directors A. James Mueller and Robert G. Zeller.)

Two North Central aircraft, the old and the new, met at the Minneapolis-St. Paul International Airport. On the left is the company's historic DC-3, "728", that had flown over 84,000 hours—more than any other aircraft in the history of aviation. In the background is the company's new 100-passenger DC-9 fan jet which entered scheduled service in September 1967.

Mechanics complete the build-up of the first DC-9, JT8D-7 fan jet engine at the company's main operations base in the Twin Cities. From left are Forrest Rathburn, Douglas instructor; North Central Mechanics William Spece, Robert Klatt and Warren Nentwig; and Lead Mechanic Donald Mitchell.

194

"Since inaugurating service," the release concluded, "North Central has carried 18.8 million passengers and flown over three billion passenger miles without a single fatality or injury to any of its passengers."

Twenty-four days after Drumm wrote those words, the most magnificent safety record in the history of U.S. aviation came to an end on a fog-blurred, rain-swept runway at Chicago O'Hare International Airport. The date was December 27; the flight was 458 from Minneapolis/St. Paul, Wausau/Marshfield, Green Bay/Clintonville, Manitowoc/Sheboygan and Milwaukee; the aircraft number was N2045; the time was 8:22 p.m. CST.

Flight 458 crashed while making an instrument approach that apparently was normal until the aircraft was a few hundred feet from the threshold of Runway 14R, at an altitude of a little more than 200 feet. At this point, the Convair 580 suddenly began to climb as Captain Marvin A. Payne initiated go-around procedures. The climb continued, however, and airspeed fell off to the point of an uncontrollable stall. The Convair smashed into the side of a hangar adjacent to the approach end of the runway. Impact occurred when the plane was nearly on its back. Of the forty-five persons aboard Flight 458, twenty-seven died—including twenty-four passengers, Captain Payne, First Officer Gerald LeValley and an additional crew member, First Officer Richard Kargel, who was riding

Milwaukee and Minot, North Dakota, won "Station of the Year" honors in 1968. Participating in the Milwaukee award ceremony are (from left) Thomas Needham, Vice President-Ground Operations; Kenneth Kiefer, Station Manager; Bernard Sweet, Executive Vice President; Wallace Skinner, Regional Passenger Service Manager; Louis Imbery, Passenger Service Manager; and David Moran, Vice President-Traffic and Sales.

Headquarters are nearly completed. Construction of North Central's new $17-million general office and main operations base, located at the Minneapolis-St. Paul International Airport, is well underway in October 1968. Plans call for occupancy of the operations base (left) by maintenance and engineering sections during the winter. The general office is to be completed later in 1969.

on the cockpit jumpseat. The twenty-eighth fatality was a person in the hangar at the time of the accident.

The National Transportation Safety Board verdict:

". . . the probable cause of this accident was spacial disorientation of the captain, precipitated by atmospheric refraction of either the approach lights or landing lights at a critical point in the approach wherein the crew was transitioning between flying by reference to flight instruments and by visual reference to the ground."

It was an old trap into which more than one pilot has fallen—that delicate moment when body, brain and eyes totally acclimated to instrument flight suddenly must shift to visual. The cockpit voice recorder contained evidence that Payne was partially blinded or confused by the fog-distorted reflections coming from either his own landing lights or the runway approach lights.

Some North Central pilots still refuse to go along with the NTSB findings. They believe Flight 458 was the victim of wake turbulence from a big jet. At the time, wake turbulence was considered hazardous only to small aircraft, but since then, planes as large as the DC-9 have been tossed out of control when caught in the powerful vortex of larger jets.

Whatever the reason for Flight 458's fate, North Central had suffered its first fatal accident—after twenty years, ten months and four days, a span in which 19,061,314 passengers had been flown in perfect safety. For the first time, the airline had to face the grim aftermath of an air tragedy—notification of next of kin, body identification, handling news media, funerals, investigation. In making all these arrangements, some mistakes occurred, but the entire airline learned from the experience.

An advertising campaign, promoting North Central's new jet service, features company personnel. From left are Captain Charles Nason, First Officer Albert Davis, Mechanic David Adams, Stewardess Kathleen Curran, Passenger Service Agent Linda Lynn (seated), Senior Station Agent John Daub, Senior Passenger Service Agent Ronald Rickey and Stewardess Jill Kilgore.

These North Central stewardesses were graduated in December 1967. They are (from left), in the back row, Peggy Gould, Elisabeth Stabell, Shirley Lundeen, Sharon Cox, Barbara Brock, and Marilyn Baldwin; center row: Nancy Hutcheson, Bonnie Higgins, Diane Wallin, Gayle Niesen, Diane Johnsen, Donna Yocum, and Sandra Pietron; front row: Nancy Warden, Bonnie Warn, Virginia Feidt, and Claudia Mercil.

"Never look back, always ahead," Schwandt had said. North Central did just that. It was on the verge of becoming an all-jet airline, and this had been made possible months before the O'Hare accident. Of the thirty-five Convairs in service, twenty-six were already modified, and the 580 had proved to be such a good airplane that Carr decided to convert the other nine. Borrowing authority was stretched as far as possible, so Dan May came up with a financing strategy. North Central went ahead with the nine conversions and sold the planes to a leasing company for $450,000 each which raised over $4 million in welcome cash. The airline then leased the planes.

The lease arrangement was used again when North Central upped the DC-9 fleet from ten to fifteen. The leasing company deposited the down payment on the additional five jets and leased them back to the airline. It was a good deal for both parties; North Central transferred large investment tax credits to the leasing company which enabled it to lease back the planes at less than the airline could have bought them.

February 7, 1969 was the big day. On that date, the final scheduled DC-3 trip was flown from the Twin Cities to Mankato, and North Central was now an all-jet airline. Like the ancient Electras before them, the DC-3s had

Stockholders gathered in Wausau, Wisconsin, for the 1968 Annual Meeting. Chairman of the Board and President Hal Carr reviews the airline's operation in the year 1967.

"Crew of the year" members for 1968, pictured with President Hal Carr, are (from left) First Officer Bob Niederer, Captain Bill Hannan, Stewardess Jean Krbechek, Carr, Captain Phil Soderlind, First Officer Gary Shutty, Stewardess Karen Sulzer, First Officer Dick Edwards, Stewardess Rita Molland, and Captain Gerald Fillmore.

done what was asked of them and more. They had moved over for the 340s and 440s, and now they had been shunted completely aside by the jets, but they would never be forgotten. They were the planes about which songs were sung and stories told and memories compiled.

Such as the grouse that hated North Central's DC-3s. Bob Ceronsky and Charlie Cox still talk about this fearless bird that used to fly interceptor missions against every DC-3 that came into Hibbing.

"Once," Ceronsky relates, "he stood smack in the middle of the runway, flapping his wings and actually defying me to land."

Ray Naddy of the Hibbing *Daily Tribune* didn't believe it when Cox told him a grouse had declared war on North Central's planes. Naddy went out to the airport and saw the bird for himself.

"His 'horns' pop out of his head as he starts his challenge dance, his yellow neck sacs inflate as he runs back and forth—his tail high, head low," Naddy wrote. Cox himself solved the mystery of the plane-hating bird. He found the grouse's girl friend parked on a nest of eggs in tall grass alongside the runway.

That's what it was like in North Central's DC-3 days, when the company's most widely-circulated publicity came from a funny little bird at a small-town airport.

Only "728", dolled up like a dowager wearing expensive clothes to hide her real age, remained as a link with the glorious past. North Central went into 1969 with ten DC-9s (five still to be delivered), thirty-four Convair 580s and 3,000 employees whose loyalty was also a link with what had gone before.

The five types of aircraft flown by North Central made a "Twentieth Anniversary Flight" over the Twin Cities area in February 1968. Leading the formation is the Lockheed 10A with which the airline started operations. Following are the Convair 340/440, introduced in 1959; the Douglas DC-9 fan jet which debuted in 1967; the DC-3, added in 1951; and the Convair 580 prop-jet, in service since 1967.

CHAPTER EIGHT

Right Approach

Artistically and potentially, 1969 was the greatest year in North Central's history, but financially, it was a flop; the company lost money for the first time since 1953. The net loss was $2.38 million even though revenues shot to an all-time high of $68.4 million—$13 million more than in 1968 and the largest revenue gain in North Central's twenty-two years. But the airline was not immune to what had hit virtually every other airline in the country—rising labor and materials cost, plus a travel market softened by the recession. Few of the trunks and none of the regional airlines made money in 1969.

Even so, North Central chalked up a modest but solid operating profit of nearly $400,000, despite a 26 percent hike in operating expenses. The red ink stemmed from the costs involved in the huge re-equipment program; interest payments alone soared to almost $5 million for the year, and depreciation on the new fleet amounted to $5.6 million.

It could have been worse without the company's strong under-pinnings—such as the continuing Operation Cold Front. The Midwest winter was unusually severe and prolonged, yet North Central's schedule completion record was over 98 percent. Of the 209,755 departures, less than one-tenth of one percent were cancelled for mechanical reasons, and only one and a half percent were delayed by mechanicals.

The heavy interest drain caused North Central to once more seek betterment of its cash position. This was achieved when the company called a special stockholders' meeting and won approval of a plan to issue six million additional shares of common stock. The sale resulted in a $9.8-million transfusion.

For the second year in a row, North Central carried over three million passengers, and more records were broken—353,907 passengers flew during

North Central Board Chairman Hal Carr cuts the official ribbon of the airline's inaugural flight from Minneapolis/St. Paul to Denver in 1969. From left are Howard Hicks, Manager-Transportation, Denver Chamber of Commerce; Colorado Lt. Governor Mark Hogan; Chan Gurney, North Central director; Carr; Stewardess Karen Forsberg and Dallas Cook, Assistant to the President of the Denver Chamber.

August for a new monthly record; the 13,619 passengers boarded on August 1 established a daily high. The financial difficulties, however serious, were dwarfed by several happier developments.

In April, the Civil Aeronautics Board awarded North Central its longest nonstop route—from the Twin Cities to Denver. Before the year was up, the CAB also had:

—Lifted operating restrictions on the Twin Cities-Chicago route, permitting nonstop flights.

—Certificated North Central for service between Milwaukee and three new Ohio cities: Columbus, Dayton and Cincinnati.

—Awarded permanent Sioux Falls-Twin Cities and Sioux City-Kansas City nonstop authority.

The route logjam had not only been broken, but the water kept pouring through. A CAB examiner recommended that North Central be allowed to operate nonstop flights from Milwaukee to New York. (His decision was made final in 1970. The Denver and New York awards added nearly 1,500 miles to the system.) It did not take very long for the new routes to prove their value; service between the Twin Cities and Denver started June 15, and in the next six months, Denver became the airline's eighth largest revenue-generating city.

With the magnificent new headquarters facility under construction and

Bernard Sweet, who joined the airline in 1948, was elected President in April 1969.

long-haul routes now realities instead of dreams, Carr was ready to further strengthen his top management team.

His title mirrored the weight of his responsibilities: Chairman of the Board, President, and General Manager. Now it was time to promote his experienced and trusted "copilot." In April 1969, acting on Carr's recommendation, the directors named Bud Sweet President. He was to be responsible for the day-to-day operation of the airline, with Carr continuing as Chairman of the Board and Chief Executive Officer.

To back up the route explosion, North Central shelled out $8 million to IBM for a new computer system known as ESCORT—Electronic System Combining Operations, Reservations, Telecommunications. Planning for the airline's entrance into the computerized reservations field had started two years before when Carr ordered an evaluation of available systems. ESCORT was tailored to North Central's needs; it not only provided "instant" reservations capability, but also retrieval of records by name and flight number. Data could be secured on the immediate operating status of North Central's 1,300 daily flight segments, plus seat availability and fares for 3,800 connecting flight segments of twenty-one other airlines. Herman now had sophisticated eyes and ears, as well as wings.

203

At the company's 1969 annual meeting in Wausau, Wisconsin, Chairman of the Board Hal Carr addresses stockholders.

The June 1969 stewardess class includes (front row, from left) Helen Rodenberg, Fran Gilchrist, Sherry Manera and Ann Stager; (middle row) Dorothy Yeshnowski, Colette Tardiff, Karen Kaslow, Lorraine Groebner, Joanne Tilley, Eileen Weisensel, Bev Leatherman, Pam Wittemann, and Kathy Dickey; (back row) Karen Tampir, Audrey Estis, Jan Flach, Bonnie Boston, Linda Huback, Diane Palaich, Debbie Abelson, and Diane Gardner.

North Central's new General Office and Main Operations Base at the Minneapolis-St. Paul International Airport was dedicated in October 1969.

The new general office and main operations base was opened officially in October 1969, although Maintenance and Engineering already had moved into its cavernous hangars in March. Weather and supplier strikes delayed the big day for the general office, but on the weekend of October 4, the move orders were issued. Employees left the old buildings on Friday and reported to work in the spanking new facilities on Monday. Floor plans had been supplied in advance, and desks were color-coded so confusion was kept to a minimum.

The bill for the new facility came to around $17 million which included capitalized interest during construction. But for this vast sum, North Central had a headquarters adequate to meet administrative and operational needs through 1980 and plenty of room to expand beyond that.

"It is," Jack Dow says with justifiable pride, "one of the few major airline facilities that wasn't obsolete the day it opened."

For versatility and practicality, it's hard to top. All interior walls except for certain corridor walls are mounted on tracks so they can be moved for necessary expansion. The entire layout was designed with department functions in mind. Samples:

—The computer room is located on the ground floor just off the lobby so visitors can see the impressive machines with their dancing, multi-colored lights.

—Public Relations is at the head of the lobby stairs on the second floor, a location dictated by the fact that it is a frequently visited department,

North Central's three-bay hangar can house nine DC-9 jets at one time or fifteen Convair 580 prop-jets. The sign is the largest in Minnesota. It stretches nearly the entire length of the 750-foot building, with letters ten feet tall.

and the same is true for Personnel, which is on the first floor just beyond the reception desk.

—The courtyard is next to the cafeteria so employees can eat outside in good weather.

—Lunch rooms are placed at each end of the main hangar to save steps. (Another time-saving innovation is the remote-controlled "driverless train"—an electric tug pulling carts on a magnetic track running through the maintenance shops. Mechanics needing parts just order them from the stockroom, and the train delivers them. A seemingly minor item, but an important one since payroll expenses are almost half of North Central's cost dollar.)

One headache Dow had was the location of the huge emergency water tank. Burying it underground would have involved high excavation and plumbing costs, and the cheaper method of putting it above ground would have had all the aesthetic appeal of a wart on a nose. The problem was solved by covering the tank with dirt and then landscaping the big mound.

The new headquarters facility and its impressive grounds won an industrial landscaping award.

The coveted Milwaukee-New York authority came through in June of 1970, along with the Omaha-Twin Cities nonstop. Putting North Central into New York involved the longest route ever granted the airline—738 miles—and the Omaha leg added another 282 miles. The system now stretched to 9,900 miles in thirteen states. And after 1969's disappointing financial record, the company did a repeat performance of its 1954 comeback: the 1970 results showed an all-time profit mark of more than $2.18 million and total revenues of nearly $92 million.

North Central Chairman of the Board Hal Carr turns on the Theme Fountain, officially dedicating the airline's new headquarters facility. President Bernard Sweet is to the left of the podium.

Dedication of the airline's new general office and main operations base attracted a large crowd, including Mayors Charles Stenvig of Minneapolis, Thomas Byrne of St. Paul, Stanley Olson of Richfield and John Thomasberg of Bloomington. Following the ceremonies, the Minneapolis/St. Paul Chambers of Commerce and Twin Cities business leaders honored the airline at a luncheon.

Milwaukee-New York nonstop service was inaugurated in September 1970. The 738-mile segment is the longest and most important single route extension ever granted to the company. Reading a congratulatory letter from New York Mayor John Lindsay are (from left) Paul Borkham, Mayor of Stevens Point, Wisconsin; Stewardess Judy Davies; and Harold Mehne, Portage County (Wisconsin) Board Chairman.

Central Wisconsin Regional Airport—serving Wausau, Stevens Point, Wisconsin Rapids and Marshfield—was opened in October 1969. Many North Central cities erected new terminals and made airport improvements to accommodate traffic growth and jet aircraft.

208

North Central began service over both the New York and Omaha routes on September 8—the former a huge success that overshadowed the latter in everything but publicity. Because so much attention was being paid to the Milwaukee-New York inauguration, Omaha played second fiddle. There was little promotion, and the first early morning nonstop took off from Omaha with just a single passenger—but when the flight arrived in the Twin Cities, the luggage was missing! In the excitement of working his first DC-9 jet, the North Central agent had simply forgotten to load the bag. The incident got more nationwide publicity than all the Milwaukee-New York fanfare could generate.

The New York route completed a revolution that the Toronto and Denver awards had started. North Central was no longer a local carrier, and definitely not the small-town, folksy airline of the past. It was literally "big time," and the demands for luxury service reflected the changing passenger pattern. The typical passenger of the Forties and Fifties was the smalltowner who used North Central for travel between cities on its system, or to connect with the trunks. Now the average passenger was a more experienced, sophisticated traveler who could well be from a larger city, and who judged the airline by the same standards he used in rating a United or American flight.

This wasn't true of all North Central's operations, of course, not when so many small communities were being served. But even a small town was only hours away from major hubs in the United States and abroad. Milwaukee, for example, emerged as a major Midwest gateway for such cities. The new Central Wisconsin Regional Airport, which opened in 1969, could now provide Wausau, Stevens Point, Wisconsin Rapids and Marshfield with single-plane service to New York, via Milwaukee. The same was true of Green Bay/Clintonville, LaCrosse and Duluth/Superior.

One thing never changed, and hopefully, never will—the fierce *esprit de corps* that has been a North Central tradition since the early days of

North Central's new circular boarding terminal opened at Milwaukee's General Mitchell Field in December 1969. The $2.5-million facility has eight upper-level gates for convenient passenger check-in and on-line transfer.

Clintonville and Madison. Not even the cosmopolitan, rule-bound atmosphere of the jet age could quell that spirit. Bill Banks demonstrated this one hot day in Chicago when a stewardess worriedly reported that not enough ice had been boarded to meet what would be a heavy demand for cold drinks.

"So get some more," Banks advised her.

"I don't know what's wrong," she said almost tearfully, "but they told me there wasn't any more ice."

"I'll be right back," Banks said.

He showed up a few minutes later with a large sack of ice. The stewardess asked no questions, and Banks volunteered no answers. For a very good reason. He had slipped unnoticed aboard another airline's plane and "appropriated" some of their ice.

Nor has North Central's informality disappeared entirely, either on the part of the airline or its passenger. Every day dozens of letters pour into the

The company's new $17-million headquarters were designed to meet administrative and operational needs through 1980 and allow for future expansion. In the foreground is the General Office, connected by a covered walkway to the Flight Kitchen/Cafeteria (directly behind) and to the Main Operations Base with its hangar area and related shops. The building in the far rear center is the company's $900,000 jet-engine test cell.

Receptionist Irene Ericson (left) greets visitors in the lobby of the new General Office.

One of the airline's three Reservations Centers (right) is located in the General Office. Reservationists use TV-like agent sets with keyboards to input and retrieve information from ESCORT, the airline's $8-million electronic reservations and communications system. Similar centers are at Milwaukee and Detroit.

Mechanics work on DC-9 fan jet engines (background) and Convair 580 prop-jet engines in the company's new Main Operations Base.

The Minneapolis and St. Paul Chambers of Commerce presented a chrome-plated DC-3 propeller to the airline in October 1969. An accompanying plaque cites North Central's contribution to the economic growth of the Twin Cities. Chairman of the Board and Chief Executive Officer Hal Carr (right) accepts the special award from Gerald Moore (left), Executive Vice President, Greater Minneapolis Chamber; and Walter Dorle, President, St. Paul Area Chamber.

ESCORT, North Central's $8-million electronic reservations and communications system, is located in the General Office adjacent to the main lobby. Two IBM 360 "real-time" computers form the heart of the system.

Francis Higgins (seated), the airline's first President, visits with North Central Director Kenneth Willett and Manager of Engineering Ralph (Stub) Roberts in 1969. Higgins came to the Twin Cities for the headquarters dedication.

general office from passengers criticizing, complimenting, giving or seeking advice. There was, for example, what has become North Central's most famous individual comment. Passenger correspondence is supervised by Marlene Krogstad, whose staff investigates and prepares hundreds of letters a month. But not even Marlene's efficient operation could adequately respond to a letter received one day in the dead of winter. The message was as follows:

"Dear Mr. Carr:

The airplane is cold
The coffee is cold
The stewardess is cold
And you're not so hot yourself."

With the flood of new route awards, Carr knew North Central was over the hump. It was not only over the hump, but several thousand feet above it. The 1970 net profit of $2.18 million was the greatest in its history. The $92 million in total revenues also smashed all records. The net profit, almost 50 percent over the previous high, was achieved in spite of a record $83.8 million in operating expenses and nearly $5 million of interest charges. This was accomplished at a time when the airline industry was not

Four North Central mechanics were awarded citations in the Federal Aviation Administration's 1969 "Mechanic of the Year" program. Presenting the awards is Roman Mueller, (center) Maintenance Section Chief of Flight Standards, FAA's District Office #34. The mechanics are (from left) Raymond Heaser, accessory overhaul; Vandon Johnson, component overhaul; Wilfred Goran, accessory overhaul; and Carl Owens, propeller overhaul.

yet fully recovered from the 1969 debacle—North Central flew into the Seventies with the best financial record of any of the regional carriers.

Two more DC-9s were delivered in 1970, bringing the jet fleet up to fifteen, with thirty-four Convair 580s flying the shorter-haul routes. The expanded fleet carried 3,753,000 passengers—another record—and it was the third consecutive year in which the three-million mark was surpassed. Traffic would have been even higher had it not been for the air traffic controller slowdown and the still-lingering effects of the sluggish economy.

North Central's splendid showing in 1970 underlined the increasing efficiency and productivity of the jets. It was possible to break even on a Milwaukee-New York flight with less than thirty-five passengers. The steadily improving financial posture also gave the airline more opportunity for big-time cabin service—with a slick inflight magazine bearing the same name as the employee newspaper, *Northliner*, that was previously carried in seat pockets. The first issue, put on planes in

New stewardess uniforms were introduced in December 1969. Modeling the ensemble, featuring apollo blue, are (from left) Judy Davies, Judy Ruff, Jill Kilgore and Fran Seidler.

214

*Members of North Central's Board of Directors are shown at their
September 1970 meeting. From left, seated, are H. P. Skoglund,
Minneapolis; G. F. DeCoursin, Dallas; Hal N. Carr, Chairman;
Samuel H. Maslon, Minneapolis; Senator Chan Gurney, Yankton,
South Dakota; and Jay Phillips, Minneapolis; (standing) Joseph E.
Rapkin, Milwaukee; Bernard Sweet, North Central President;
Kenneth B. Willett, Stevens Point, Wisconsin; and Morton B.
Phillips, Minneapolis.*

October, had a full-color picture of a mallard duck on the cover—an
appropriate tribute to Herman.

North Central reached a magic mark in 1971 when total revenues hit
$100 million, with net profits of $1.2 million. The passenger count neared
the four-million level as 3,793,000 persons were carried. A completion
record of 99 percent of scheduled mileage was achieved, with on-time
performance at a highly satisfactory 81.4 percent.

ESCORT utilization was expanded. Hiring guidelines were revised to
provide employment for disadvantaged minority groups. New takeoff
procedures were devised to reduce aircraft noise up to 50 percent without
compromising safety. Another step toward making North Central a good
environmental neighbor, as well as a means of transportation, was taken
with the conversion of all DC-9 engines to "smokeless" operation. It was
costly—some $300,000—but the retrofit not only eliminated visible
pollutants but reduced invisible emissions by 23 percent.

The environmental efforts were even extended into maintenance
procedures. Outdoor engine testing was eliminated from 11 p.m. to 6 a.m.

Stewardess class graduates in December 1970 were (front row, from left) Linda Wales, Romalee Rule, Doris Massman, Sandra Daugaard and Louise Marvin; (back row) Trudy Cross, Judy Brawner, Karen Kuemmerlin, Lorraine Bell, Krecia Thompson, Karen Prins, Kathy Olslund, Linda Skedgell, Cecilia Byrne, Phillis Bonner, Suzanne Schroeder, Eva Woods, and Starr Skyberg.

North Central passenger service agents model new navy-and-persimmon uniforms introduced in May 1971. From left are Vickie Fischer, John Hollenstein, Virginia DeBose, Adriane Briganti, Ted Messmore and Phyllis Ware.

Civil Aeronautics Board Chairman Secor Browne (left) meets with Hal Carr, North Central Chairman of the Board, in September 1971. Browne visited the airline's headquarters in Minneapolis/St. Paul.

North Central also uses cleaning and maintenance products that are easily decomposed by natural elements. Water purification in heating-plant boilers is now accomplished with environmentally approved chemicals. Aircraft and ground equipment are washed with emulsion-type biodegradable soaps. Even "Cold Front" got into the act with the adoption of the most disposable de-icing fluids.

"The company," Carr emphasized, "is making every effort to be a compatible neighbor and business partner in the communities it serves."

So, for that matter, were the communities themselves. In addition to the new Central Wisconsin Airport, major airport improvements were completed at Green Bay, Yankton, Pellston, Flint, Sioux Falls and Milwaukee. And the mushrooming charter business sent little Herman's wings humming over cities far off its route system—Acapulco, Mexico City, Montreal, San Juan, Nassau, Washington, D.C., San Francisco, and Las Vegas. Charter flights in 1971 totaled 459, a figure which did not include 153 scenic flights that introduced North Central to nearly 10,000 potential new customers.

The year 1971 was one of consolidation, plus a setting of the stage for the future; and 1972 was a continuation of this quietly confident mood. For 1972 was North Central's twenty-fifth year—a time to look back as well as ahead. But it was marred on June 29 by the airline's second fatal crash, yet one which involved an incredible coincidence.

A Convair 580 on Flight 290 from Green Bay, delayed more than two

Vice President of Industrial Relations Arthur Schwandt receives his 25-year service pin from Chairman of the Board Hal Carr in February 1972. Schwandt, one of the original directors of Wisconsin Central, served as an officer throughout his entire career with the airline.

hours by weather, was cleared by the tower for landing at Oshkosh. At 10:37 a.m. over Lake Winnebago, the aircraft collided with an Air Wisconsin Otter, running thirteen minutes late, which was on approach to the airport at Appleton. Two passengers were on the North Central plane plus the crew, Captain James Cuzzort, First Officer Alton Laabs, and Stewardess Frances Rabb; there were no survivors. The air taxi plane was carrying six passengers and two pilots, all of whom perished.

As 1972 progressed, it became apparent that the company's forecasts for the year and all previous traffic records would be far exceeded. The airline was realizing excellent passenger gains on its long-haul routes, and the improved general economy helped stimulate traffic. For the first nine months, 3,282,000 passengers were carried, and the company proudly reported profits of $5,383,000. Orders were placed for three new DC-9s to be delivered in 1973, and the future looked rosy.

Just before the end of the year, however, disaster struck again in the form of an unavoidable accident. On the evening of December 20, a North

Centenarian Sarah Hellstrom made her very first plane trip September 19, 1971, when she flew on North Central from Minneapolis/St. Paul to Brainerd, Minnesota. Mrs. Hellstrom, who was nearly 101 years old, receives a corsage of roses from Stewardess Terry Miller.

Jack Benny (forever 39) pauses to chat with Mike Furlong, North Central traffic and sales manager in Toronto, before boarding a flight to Detroit in April 1972.

The 1971 award for "outstanding landscaping and maintenance" was presented to North Central by the Men's Garden Club of Minneapolis. The grounds, like those around the Flight Kitchen/ Employee Cafeteria (below), were described as "far superior to any others for the entire growing season."

Stewardess Sue Carter, Captain Charles Timberg and First Officer Rupert Thompson prepare for a flight.

James W. Hoeschler (second from right), President, Hoeschler Realty Corporation, LaCrosse, was named a North Central Presidential Advisor in April 1972. Taking part in the event were airline President Bernard Sweet and Stewardesses Sandy Pietron (left) and Rosemary Vick.

Quotabuster Station of the Year honors for 1972 were presented by Manager of Sales Administration Bill Runnels to Rochester, Minnesota; Milwaukee; and Sioux Falls, South Dakota. Participating in ceremonies at Rochester are (from left) Station Agent Rodney Plath, Runnels, Agents John Standke and Robert Benson, Manager Vernon Beyer and Agent Leroy Johnson.

Central DC-9 on Flight 575, cleared by the O'Hare airport tower for takeoff, was halfway down the runway and barely airborne when a Delta Convair 880 suddenly loomed out of the fog. Visibility was only a quarter of a mile, and the Delta jet, under ground control, was taxiing across the active runway.

North Central had its third fatal crash in twenty-five years of operation. The two aircraft collided. Of the forty-one passengers and four crew members aboard the DC-9, ten passengers were killed. On the Delta Convair, several passengers were injured, but there were no fatalities.

Even before the National Transportation Safety Board released its decision placing the blame for the accident, it was immediately clear that North Central was not at fault. In a statement published the day after the crash, an FAA spokesman was quoted as saying, "The big question is why the Delta pilot was even on that runway. There are only two explanations—either the pilot goofed or the control tower goofed."

Company employees who were with the airline when operations began February 24, 1948, gathered for a Twenty-Fifth Anniversary Dinner in 1973. Standing are (from left) Gale Lorsbach, Pete Petit, Joe DeCoursin, John Downing, Don Planck, Chuck Nason, Bob Gren, Matt Ruper, Ken Schuck, Charlie Cox, Bill Banks, Art Hinke, Jack Starry, Dick Cooper, Gordon Torkelson, George Roycraft, Joe Sims, Bob Allison, Ray Miller, Myron Broten, Magnus Budzien, Oscar Malotky, Pete Hofman, Walt Kneller, Ken Sersland, and Frank Seitz. Sitting are (from left) Bob Ceronsky, Tom Needham, Ralph Parkinson, Karl Brocken, Milt Ellyson, Hal Carr, Jim Grant, Lloyd Franke, Bob Swennes, and George Bell. (Not shown are Harold Ebelt, Hal Picquet, Arthur Schwandt and Francis Higgins.)

As Hal Carr wrote to his directors at the time, "It is small consolation to know that our aircraft was operating strictly in accordance with instructions from the tower, and our people were in no way at fault. There are, of course, inherent risks in all forms of transportation, but tragic occurrences such as this are the heartbreaking part of an otherwise fascinating business."

North Central ended the year 1972 in a blaze of traffic and financial glory. The Annual Report to Stockholders indicated that the company's total revenues reached a record $120,627,000, with a net profit of $7,536,000—the highest earnings in North Central's 25-year history. The airline carried 4,318,643 passengers over a billion passenger miles, and twelve million ton miles of mail, express, and freight were flown.

222

Looking back with a kind of quiet pride in what has been accomplished, Carr sums up his nineteen-year stewardship of the airline with a simple, "I guess we're in good shape now."

And that is an understatement. North Central has operated profitably for eighteen of the nineteen years that Carr has headed the company, something no other regional carrier can say, and for that matter, few of the trunklines. What is merely "good shape" applies to an airline that, on the basis of debt/equity ratio and retained earnings, is among the financially strongest airlines in the industry. North Central is, in fact, one of the two regional carriers with any retained earnings—$14,262,000 at the end of 1972.

In the company's day-to-day operation, Bud Sweet continues in the same pattern as Carr—running a closely-knit, cost-conscious airline that never forgets the famine of the Forties even as it dines well in the

Comedian Bob Hope flew to Mankato in August 1972 on "728", North Central's corporate DC-3 cited for having flown more hours than any other aircraft in the history of aviation. Entertainer Helena Jackson is at left, with Stewardess Suzanne Swenson behind Hope.

Jack Bowen, (right) representing Chicago Mayor Richard Daley, presented the city flag to crew members on North Central's 25th Anniversary Flight in February 1973. From left are Captain Ralph Parkinson, Chicago Base Stewardess Supervisor Mary Ann Swanger, Captain Bob Ceronsky, Stewardess Suzanne Swenson and Captain Art Hinke. The captains, all members of the original pilot group, used corporate aircraft "728" to reenact North Central's first scheduled flights over its 1,028-mile route system of 1948.

Seventies, with a management team that respects its responsibilities to employees and its obligation to make money for the stockholders. North Central has never had a strike, thanks partially to Art Schwandt's tough but fair bargaining skill and partially to management's policy of stopping trouble before it grows into ugly ill will.

When questioned as to the reasons for North Central's success, officials of other airlines attribute it to several factors. Those frequently mentioned include dependable service, continuous upgrading of flight equipment and facilities, superior operating performance, aggressive route development, and astute long-range planning—in other words, the right approach: sound corporate management.

In retrospect, North Central's chances of developing into a major airline were infinitely remote. Of the nearly 1,600 parties which had sought CAB certificates in the 1940s, only nineteen new airlines were authorized. Two of these were never able to start service, nine were merged or absorbed by other carriers, and today there are just eight surviving regional airlines. Literally, the odds against the company's succeeding were about 200 to 1.

North Central's people are all tremendously proud of the airline they have built. But it is safe to say they are not yet content.

And that not only sums up the long, torturous road from the airline's humble beginnings in Clintonville to a $120-million corporation, it also lays the groundwork for North Central's next twenty-five years of progress—with ceiling and visibility unlimited.

A North Central DC-9 fan jet takes off over the terminal building at the Minneapolis-St. Paul International Airport. The airline enters its second twenty-five years with a fleet of eighteen DC-9s and thirty-three Convair 580 prop-jets.

Acknowledgments

The author would like to express his appreciation to the many officers and employees of North Central Airlines who took time away from their tasks for the interviews and research aid that made this book possible.

In most cases, their names are included in the history itself. But I would like to pay special thanks to Hal Carr, Bud Sweet, Charlotte Westberg, Bob Hall, Dorothy Bradshaw and Jon Harty for help above and beyond the call of duty.

To Mr. and Mrs. Francis Higgins for a hospitable and informative visit, my gratitude.

And finally, my deep appreciation to Del Drumm who conceived the project and aided immeasurably in its completion. This book deserves his byline as much as my own.

The majority of source material came from personal interviews and the company's archives which are now part of the Northliner Museum. I wish to acknowledge also the courtesy of Eric Bramley in supplying me with his own files on North Central.

Robert J. Serling

About the Author

Robert J. Serling, a former aviation editor of United Press International, has covered commercial aviation for nearly thirty years. He is the author of six books—three novels and three nonfiction— including the best-selling *The President's Plane is Missing*. His latest novel, *She'll Never Get Off the Ground,* is the story of a woman airline pilot, and is being made into a television movie.

Serling is a seven-time winner of TWA's Best Aviation News Reporting Award and has been cited for his contributions to public understanding of air safety problems by the Aviation/Space Writers Association, the Flight Safety Foundation, the Sherman Fairchild Foundation and the Air Line Pilots Association.

He resides in Potomac, Maryland, with his wife Priscilla (a former stewardess), their daughter Jennifer and son Jeffrey.

APPENDICES

APPENDIX I
DIRECTORS

APPENDIX II
OFFICERS

APPENDIX III
PRESIDENTIAL ADVISORS

Directors

WALTER A. OLEN	May 15, 1944 - January 30, 1946
FRANCIS M. HIGGINS	May 15, 1944 - October 14, 1952
HERBERT S. FOTH	May 15, 1944 - May 19, 1948
GARNET F. DeCOURSIN	May 15, 1944 - Present
ARTHUR E. SCHWANDT	May 15, 1944 - January 14, 1948 April 23, 1952 - October 14, 1952
PERCY V. CHAFFEE	May 15, 1944 - January 8, 1946
BERNARD O. STIEG	May 15, 1944 - March 20, 1947
EMIL C. GEHRKE	May 15, 1944 - May 19, 1948
DONALD B. OLEN	January 30, 1946 - April 1, 1953
ROBERT J. OYAAS	May 15, 1946 - May 21, 1947
WILLIAM A. ROBERTS	February 15, 1947 - May 19, 1948
HARRY B. HALL	March 20, 1947 - January 14, 1948
FRED V. GARDNER	September 10, 1947 - April 23, 1952
MILO F. SNYDER	January 14, 1948 - April 23, 1952
HOWARD A. MOREY	January 14, 1948 - April 7, 1954
ARTHUR T. SPENCE	May 19, 1948 - July 14, 1949
G. EDWARD SLEZAK	May 19, 1948 - April 23, 1952
ARTHUR E. A. MUELLER	May 19, 1948 - March 15, 1965
A. L. WHEELER	July 14, 1949 - May 24, 1963
HAL N. CARR	April 23, 1952 - Present
HAROLD H. EMCH, SR.	April 23, 1952 - April 7, 1954

233

ROBERT B. STEWART	October 14, 1952 - November 19, 1954
GROVE WEBSTER	April 1, 1953 - December 10, 1954
WERNER L. CHRISTENSEN	April 1, 1953 - December 3, 1965
KENNETH B. WILLETT	April 7, 1954 - Present
ROBERT F. GROVER	April 7, 1954 - April 2, 1958
CHARLES R. HOOD	April 2, 1958 - January 21, 1961
A. JAMES MUELLER	April 5, 1961 - April 2, 1969
DAVID E. CROOKER	April 5, 1961 - June 9, 1970
H. P. SKOGLUND	September 25, 1964 - Present
JOSEPH E. RAPKIN	March 26, 1965 - Present
ROBERT G. ZELLER	December 3, 1965 - January 23, 1970
CHAN GURNEY	April 6, 1966 - Present
SAMUEL H. MASLON	April 6, 1966 - Present
JAY PHILLIPS	April 6, 1966 - Present
MORTON B. PHILLIPS	April 6, 1966 - Present
BERNARD SWEET	April 2, 1969 - Present

Officers

FRANCIS M. HIGGINS	President	May 15, 1944 - October 14, 1952
HERBERT S. FOTH	Vice President	May 15, 1944 - May 19, 1948
BERNARD O. STIEG	Treasurer	May 15, 1944 - March 20, 1947
ARTHUR E. SCHWANDT	Secretary	May 15, 1944 - May 16, 1945
	Secretary and Assistant Treasurer	May 16, 1945 - March 20, 1947
	Secretary-Treasurer	March 20, 1947 - May 1, 1953
	Vice President and Secretary	May 1, 1953 - November 1, 1954
	Vice President-Industrial Relations	November 1, 1954 - April 22, 1973
HAL N. CARR	Vice President-Traffic	May 15, 1947 - January 14, 1948
	Executive Vice President	January 14, 1948 - March 15, 1952
	President and General Manager	April 7, 1954 - March 26, 1965
	Chairman of the Board and President	March 26, 1965 - April 2, 1969
	Chairman of the Board and Chief Executive Officer	April 2, 1969 - Present
A. IRVINE PETT	Vice President-Operations	May 21, 1947 - April 5, 1948
ROBERT D. GARDNER	Assistant Treasurer	January 1, 1948 - March 10, 1948
A. L. WHEELER	Vice President and Counsel	July 14, 1949 - May 24, 1963
BERNARD SWEET	Assistant Treasurer	November 26, 1950 - May 1, 1953
	Acting Treasurer	May 1, 1953 - November 19, 1954
	Secretary-Treasurer	November 19, 1954 - April 1, 1959
	Vice President and Secretary-Treasurer	April 1, 1959 - April 5, 1961
	Vice President and Treasurer	April 5, 1961 - April 3, 1963
	Vice President-Finance	April 3, 1963 - April 5, 1967
	Executive Vice President	April 5, 1967 - April 2, 1969
	President	April 2, 1969 - Present
DELMAR G. HENDRICKSON	Vice President-Operations and Maintenance	August 9, 1951 - June 30, 1952

FRANK N. BUTTOMER	Vice President-Traffic and Sales	August 9, 1951 - November 24, 1966
HOWARD A. MOREY	Vice President President and General Manager	April 23, 1952 - January 1, 1953 January 1, 1953 - March 9, 1954
DONALD A. DUFF	Executive Vice President and General Manager	May 15, 1952 - November 14, 1952
ARTHUR E. A. MUELLER	Chairman of the Board President	April 23, 1952 - March 15, 1965 October 14, 1952 - January 1, 1953
GROVE WEBSTER	Vice President	October 14, 1952 - December 10, 1954
ALVIN D. NIEMEYER	Vice President-Flight Operations	April 6, 1955 - July 31, 1966
R.H. BENDIO, SR.	Vice President-Maintenance and Engineering	April 6, 1955 - September 30, 1967
JOHN P. DOW	Assistant Secretary Secretary Vice President and Secretary	April 1, 1959 - April 5, 1961 April 5, 1961 - September 22, 1967 September 22, 1967 - Present
CHARLOTTE G. WESTBERG	Assistant Secretary	April 4, 1962 - Present
DANIEL F. MAY	Assistant Treasurer Treasurer Vice President and Treasurer Vice President-Finance	April 4, 1962 - April 6, 1963 April 6, 1963 - September 22, 1967 September 22, 1967 - December 3, 1971 December 3, 1971 - Present
DELMAR F. DRUMM	Assistant Secretary	April 8, 1964 - April 7, 1965
JERROLD SCOUTT, JR.	Assistant Secretary	April 8, 1964 - April 6, 1966
LESLIE J. KEELY	Vice President-Maintenance and Engineering	April 7, 1965 - January 28, 1972
THOMAS M. NEEDHAM	Vice President-Ground Operations	April 7, 1965 - Present
GAILE F. WALLIS	Vice President-Flight Operations	April 7, 1965 - Present
GOWAN J. MILLER	Assistant Secretary Vice President-Industrial Relations	April 6, 1966 - May 25, 1973 May 25, 1973 - Present
DAVID E. MORAN	Vice President-Traffic and Sales	September 22, 1967 - Present
JAMES F. NIXON	Assistant Treasurer Treasurer	April 8, 1970 - December 3, 1971 December 3, 1971 - Present
ROBERT L. GREN	Vice President-Maintenance and Engineering	January 26, 1973 - Present
GEORGE J. KARNAS	Vice President-Inflight Service	April 4, 1973 - Present

236

Presidential Advisors

CARL N. JACOBS	President Hardware Mutuals Stevens Point, Wisconsin	*(October 12, 1954)*
ROBERT ALDRICH	Executive Director Minneapolis-St. Paul Metropolitan Airports Commission St. Paul, Minnesota	*(October 18, 1954)*
L. L. SCHROEDER	Commissioner Minnesota Department of Aeronautics St. Paul, Minnesota	*(October 18, 1954)*
JOSEPH HORNER, JR.	Business Manager *The Press-Gazette* Green Bay, Wisconsin	*(October 21, 1954)*
HAROLD A. SAGE	Manager Hotel Scott Hancock, Michigan	*(October 25, 1954)*
STEPHEN H. HARRINGTON	Assistant to the President Brown & Bigelow St. Paul, Minnesota	*(October 25, 1954)*
ELMER J. BORNHOEFT	General Superintendent Postal Transportation Service U. S. Post Office Department St. Paul, Minnesota	*(October 26, 1954)*
ANTHONY B. RONZANI	Postal Transportation Service U. S. Post Office Department St. Paul, Minnesota	*(October 26, 1954)*
ROBERT MURPHY	City Editor *The Herald-Leader* Menominee, Michigan	*(October 28, 1954)*
HERBERT J. NORTON	Chairman Michigan Aeronautics Commission Escanaba, Michigan	*(October 28, 1954)*
STEWARD D. SHELDON	President First National Bank International Falls, Minnesota	*(October 28, 1954)*

RAYMOND NOVOTNY	Postmaster Oshkosh, Wisconsin	*(November 4, 1954)*
WALTER G. ROEHL	Executive Secretary Chamber of Commerce Wausau, Wisconsin	*(November 4, 1954)*
J. J. PHILLIPS	Traffic Manager Beloit Iron Works Beloit, Wisconsin	*(November 8, 1954)*
JOHN C. FREDENDALL	Manager Rock County Airport Janesville, Wisconsin	*(November 8, 1954)*
ROBERT A. OLEN	President The Four Wheel Drive Auto Company Clintonville, Wisconsin	*(November 9, 1954)*
WALTER A. OLEN	Clintonville, Wisconsin	*(November 9, 1954)*
TED COLE	Postmaster Cashton, Wisconsin	*(November 10, 1954)*
W. F. WIELAND	Chairman Crow Wing County Airport Commission Brainerd, Minnesota	*(November 10, 1954)*
B. H. YOUNG	President Wisconsin Chapter National Association of Postmasters Chippewa Falls, Wisconsin	*(November 10, 1954)*
ROBERT B. SKULDT	Superintendent Municipal Airport Madison, Wisconsin	*(November 22, 1954)*
T. K. JORDAN	Director Wisconsin State Aeronautics Commission Madison, Wisconsin	*(November 22, 1954)*
H. FRANK MUTH	Manager Municipal Airport La Crosse, Wisconsin	*(November 23, 1954)*
BRADLEY R. TAYLOR	Rhinelander, Wisconsin	*(November 23, 1954)*
WARREN S. PARR	Rear Admiral, USN (ret) Washington, D. C.	*(December 1, 1954)*
ERIC BRAMLEY	Vice President American Aviation Publications, Inc. Washington, D. C.	*(December 30, 1954)*
JOSEPH FONTANA	Manager Ford Airport Iron Mountain, Michigan	*(January 6, 1955)*
MARIO FONTANA	President Fontana Aviation Company Iron Mountain, Michigan	*(January 6, 1955)*
EARL O. OLSON	Manager Municipal Airport Duluth, Minnesota	*(January 11, 1955)*
JOHN A. AINLEY	Editor-Publisher *The Daily Pioneer* Bemidji, Minnesota	*(February 8, 1955)*

ED W. BUTLER	President KBUN Bemidji, Minnesota	*(February 8, 1955)*
JAMES A. DENEEN	City Manager Bemidji, Minnesota	*(February 8, 1955)*
JIM STOUT	Chairman, Aviation Committee Civic & Commerce Association Bemidji, Minnesota	*(February 8, 1955)*
DON STUBBINS	Executive Manager Civic & Commerce Association Bemidji, Minnesota	*(February 8, 1955)*
FRED H. SENSIBA	Manager Municipal Airport Escanaba, Michigan	*(February 11, 1955)*
KENNETH L. GUNDERMAN	Editor *Escanaba Press* Escanaba, Michigan	*(February 11, 1955)*
GEORGE M. FISHER	Executive Editor *Hibbing Daily Tribune* Hibbing, Minnesota	*(February 23, 1955)*
HELMER OLSON	Executive Manager Chamber of Commerce Hibbing, Minnesota	*(February 23, 1955)*
STEVE SHALBRECK	Manager Oneida County Airport Rhinelander, Wisconsin	*(March 11, 1955)*
CLIFFORD G. FERRIS	Executive Editor *The Rhinelander Daily News* Rhinelander, Wisconsin	*(March 25, 1955)*
JAMES L. McCARTHY	Manager Municipal Airport Stevens Point, Wisconsin	*(March 30, 1955)*
CARL S. WALLACE	Manager Chamber of Commerce Stevens Point, Wisconsin	*(March 30, 1955)*
HENRY L. YULGA	City Comptroller Stevens Point, Wisconsin	*(March 30, 1955)*
BRIG. GEN. L. J. MAITLAND	Director of Aeronautics State of Michigan Lansing, Michigan	*(April 13, 1955)*
NEIL G. BRACKSTONE	Manager Capital City Airport Lansing, Michigan	*(April 13, 1955)*
H. L. ANDERSON	Titan Chain Saws Wakefield, Michigan	*(April 18, 1955)*
A. E. WALKER	M. A. Hanna Company Iron River, Michigan	*(May 1, 1955)*
CARL E. STEIGER	President Deltox Rug Company Oshkosh, Wisconsin	*(May 9, 1955)*
S. J. WITTMAN	Manager Winnebago County Airport Oshkosh, Wisconsin	*(May 9, 1955)*

239

THOMAS WALSH	Manager Kent County Airport Grand Rapids, Michigan	*(May 23, 1955)*
ROBERT E. MILLER	President Airlines National Terminal Service Co. Willow Run Airport Ypsilanti, Michigan	*(June 1, 1955)*
COL. C. V. BURNETT	Director Detroit Aviation Commission Detroit, Michigan	*(June 1, 1955)*
DOMINIC F. VALELLA	Manager K. I. Sawyer Airport Marquette, Michigan	*(June 21, 1955)*
ROBERT B. MORRIS	Executive Secretary Duluth Chamber of Commerce Duluth, Minnesota	*(July 7, 1955)*
ALBERT NELSON	Chairman, Aviation Committee Duluth Chamber of Commerce Duluth, Minnesota	*(July 7, 1955)*
DALTON LeMASURIER	President KDAL-TV Duluth, Minnesota	*(July 7, 1955)*
D. CLARK EVEREST	Chairman of the Board Marathon Corporation Rothschild, Wisconsin	*(August 22, 1955)*
HON. MELVIN R. LAIRD	House of Representatives Washington, D.C.	*(September 13, 1955)*
WILLIAM G. WHYTE	Chairman of the Board First American State Bank Wausau, Wisconsin	*(November 2, 1955)*
WALTER F. OLSON	Vice President-Manager 20th Century Associated Grocers, Inc. Ironwood, Michigan	*(November 10, 1955)*
WILLIAM B. FAUHL	Auditor Gogebic County Bessemer, Michigan	*(November 10, 1955)*
G. H. STORDOCK	National Vice Commander The American Legion King, Wisconsin	*(December 7, 1955)*
J. ADDINGTON WAGNER	National Commander The American Legion Battle Creek, Michigan	*(December 22, 1955)*
ROBERT L. HAMILTON	President The Dumore Company Racine, Wisconsin	*(March 1, 1956)*
HOWARD O. PIHL	Secretary-Treasurer The Louis Allis Company Milwaukee, Wisconsin	*(March 1, 1956)*
FRANCIS J. TRECKER	President Kearney & Trecker Corporation Milwaukee, Wisconsin	*(March 1, 1956)*
CLARENCE J. MUTH	Manager, Air Service Division The Association of Commerce Milwaukee, Wisconsin	*(March 1, 1956)*

240

LAWRENCE J. TIMMERMAN	Chairman County Board of Supervisors Milwaukee, Wisconsin	*(March 1, 1956)*
MARSHALL STRAUS	President Straus Printing Company Madison, Wisconsin	*(March 2, 1956)*
WILLIAM E. DAHLQUIST	Editor *Thief River Falls Times* Thief River Falls, Minnesota	*(March 22, 1956)*
JAMES M. ROCHE	Secretary Chamber of Commerce Thief River Falls, Minnesota	*(March 22, 1956)*
H. J. DOW	President Louis F. Dow Company St. Paul, Minnesota	*(April 30, 1956)*
WENDELL T. BURNS	Senior Vice President Northwestern National Bank Minneapolis, Minnesota	*(June 12, 1956)*
WENDELL L. McELDOWNEY	Hilltop Farm West Salem, Wisconsin	*(July 25, 1956)*
ARLIE M. MUCKS, JR.	Manager Industrial Wholesale Division Madison Chamber of Commerce Madison, Wisconsin	*(July 26, 1956)*
KENNETH W. HAAGENSEN	Director of Public Relations Allis-Chalmers Manufacturing Co. West Allis, Wisconsin	*(September 28, 1956)*
GORDON R. CLOSWAY	Executive Editor *The Winona Daily News* Winona, Minnesota	*(October 30, 1956)*
WILLIAM E. GALEWSKI	Winona Heating and Ventilating Co. Winona, Minnesota	*(October 30, 1956)*
JOHN W. RICE	Publisher *The Daily Mining Gazette* Houghton, Michigan	*(November 7, 1956)*
CLARENCE STURM	General Manager Sturm Bros. Produce Company Manawa, Wisconsin	*(November 19, 1956)*
ALBERT T. RIDINGER	President Metallurgical, Inc. Minneapolis, Minnesota	*(January 8, 1957)*
J. R. NORTH	Vice President Commonwealth Associates, Inc. Jackson, Michigan	*(May 20, 1957)*
PAUL G. GLENKEY	Signal Electric Division King-Seeley Corporation Menominee, Michigan	*(November 5, 1957)*
CHARLES F. EIKEL, JR.	Executive Vice President CUNA Mutual Insurance Society Madison, Wisconsin	*(November 13, 1957)*
C. J. BURRILL	Manager, Transportation Department Chamber of Commerce Omaha, Nebraska	*(December 17, 1957)*

F. L. ZELL	Director of Public Relations Clark Oil and Refining Company Milwaukee, Wisconsin	*(February 5, 1958)*
H. H. MARTIN	Executive Vice President Merchants State Bank Rhinelander, Wisconsin	*(February 7, 1958)*
WILLIAM M. PACKER	President Detroit Aviation Commission Detroit, Michigan	*(April 4, 1958)*
A. S. CORWIN	Traffic Manager Oldsmobile Division General Motors Corporation Detroit, Michigan	*(April 4, 1958)*
WILLIAM MARA	Director of Advertising and Public Relations Bendix Aviation Corporation Detroit, Michigan	*(April 4, 1958)*
JAMES D. RAMSEY	Director Michigan Department of Aeronautics Lansing, Michigan	*(April 4, 1958)*
EMMONS W. COLLINS	Executive Vice President First & American National Bank Duluth, Minnesota	*(May 27, 1958)*
H. WARNER GRIGGS	Vice President Northern City National Bank Duluth, Minnesota	*(May 27, 1958)*
GEORGE W. WELLES, JR.	President Marshall Wells-Kelley How Thomson Co. Duluth, Minnesota	*(May 27, 1958)*
THOMAS C. MacCALLA, JR.	Sales Engineer Aircraft Division Eaton Manufacturing Company Battle Creek, Michigan	*(June 17, 1958)*
PHILIP H. ORDWAY	President Union Steam Pump Company Battle Creek, Michigan	*(June 17, 1958)*
EARL T. WINGET	President Kickernick, Inc. Minneapolis, Minnesota	*(July 11, 1958)*
DONALD E. SEMLING	President Wisconsin Window Unit Company Merrill, Wisconsin	*(September 25, 1958)*
A. S. KROMER	Vice President and General Manager Calumet Division Calumet & Hecla, Inc. Calumet, Michigan	*(December 2, 1958)*
H. H. HERBERGER	Secretary-Treasurer Herberger, Inc. Grand Forks, North Dakota	*(August 27, 1959)*
ROBERT E. LINDMARK	President BenCo Ophthalmic Laboratories Milwaukee, Wisconsin	*(January 27, 1960)*

LAWRENCE J. FITZPATRICK	President J. J. Fitzpatrick Lumber Company, Inc. Madison, Wisconsin	*(July 12, 1960)*
HON. JOHN A. BLATNIK	House of Representatives Washington, D.C.	*(July 29, 1960)*
C. D. TULLY	Assistant Manager *Duluth Herald and News-Tribune* Duluth, Minnesota	*(November 2, 1960)*
DAVID A. YUENGER	Managing Editor *Green Bay Press-Gazette* Green Bay, Wisconsin	*(March 28, 1961)*
DR. IRVING E. SCHIEK, SR.	Schiek Clinic Rhinelander, Wisconsin	*(May 25, 1961)*
LINCOLN B. FRAZIER	President Campbell Supply Company Marquette, Michigan	*(December 12, 1961)*
D. G. HENDRICKSON	Hendrickson Aeromar, Inc. Bahia Mar Yacht Basin Fort Lauderdale, Florida	*(March 26, 1962)*
R. C. DOBSON	Publisher *Minot Daily News* Minot, North Dakota	*(June 18, 1962)*
WILLARD MURPHY	Willard Murphy Investment Securities Chippewa Falls, Wisconsin	*(July 26, 1962)*
JEAN WORTH	Editor *Escanaba Daily Press* Escanaba, Michigan	*(August 8, 1962)*
ROYAL D. ALWORTH, JR.	Vice President and Treasurer Oneida Realty Company Duluth, Minnesota	*(August 13, 1962)*
ALEXANDER PHILLIPS	General Manager Northwestern Ontario Development Association Port Arthur, Ontario, Canada	*(August 13, 1962)*
REAR ADM. IRA H. NUNN, USN	Commandant Ninth Naval District Great Lakes, Illinois	*(January 21, 1963)*
WRIGLEY OFFIELD	Vice President-Director Wm. Wrigley, Jr. Company Chicago, Illinois	*(July 16, 1963)*
ROBERT J. RICH	General Manager WDSM Radio & TV Duluth, Minnesota	*(February 3, 1964)*
G. EMORY SIPPLE	National Vice Commander The American Legion Menomonie, Wisconsin	*(February 22, 1964)*
JOHN M. ROSE	President Kellogg Citizens National Bank Green Bay, Wisconsin	*(April 23, 1964)*
FRANCIS P. BEFERA	President Hibbing Broadcasting Co.-WMFG Hibbing, Minnesota	*(October 14, 1964)*

243

JOHN M. GANNON	Attorney at Law Hibbing, Minnesota	*(April 24, 1965)*
GLENN L. HUMPHREY	President Humphrey Enterprises Milwaukee, Wisconsin	*(June 29, 1966)*
MISS VEDA PONIKVAR	Publisher and Editor *Free Press and Tribune Press* Chisholm, Minnesota	*(August 12, 1966)*
BYRON W. REEVE	President Lake Shore, Inc. Iron Mountain, Michigan	*(September 20, 1966)*
HERBERT S. FOTH	Chairman of the Board Foth & Porath, Inc. Green Bay, Wisconsin	*(November 9, 1966)*
GEORGE S. DOUGLAS	Manager, Escanaba Division The Mead Corporation Escanaba, Michigan	*(November 9, 1966)*
WILLIAM P. NICHOLLS	Vice President Copper Range Company Houghton, Michigan	*(November 10, 1966)*
CHARLES D. GELATT	Chairman of the Board The Microcard Corporation West Salem, Wisconsin	*(December 5, 1966)*
JOSEPH L. FLOYD	President Midcontinent Broadcasting Company Sioux Falls, South Dakota	*(December 7, 1966)*
HENRY J. SCHMITT	President and Publisher Aberdeen News Company Aberdeen, South Dakota	*(May 23, 1967)*
JAMES L. VANCE	Editor *Worthington Daily Globe* Worthington, Minnesota	*(June 28, 1967)*
C. STRATTON MARTIN	Manager, Wisconsin River Division Consolidated Papers, Inc. Stevens Point, Wisconsin	*(December 6, 1967)*
JOHN E. SPOHN	General Distribution Manager Oscar Mayer & Company Madison, Wisconsin	*(December 7, 1967)*
DUTTON BROOKFIELD	President Unitog Company Kansas City, Missouri	*(May 20, 1968)*
JAMES L. MADDEN	President and General Manager Madden Bros., Inc. Brainerd, Minnesota	*(June 21, 1968)*
ROBERT A. BATDORFF	President Herald & Record Co. Traverse City, Michigan	*(July 1, 1968)*
JIM GILMORE, JR.	President Gilmore Broadcasting Corporation Kalamazoo, Michigan	*(July 2, 1968)*
GEORGE R. KERR	Attorney at Law Schacht, Kerr and Steiner Rochester, Minnesota	*(May 21, 1969)*

244

DR. JOHN N. SIMONS	Mayo Clinic Rochester, Minnesota	*(May 21, 1969)*
RICHARD D. DUDLEY	President Forward Communications Corporation Wausau, Wisconsin	*(June 4, 1969)*
LaVERNE T. LAUSTSEN	President Dakota-North Plains Corporation Aberdeen, South Dakota	*(February 17, 1970)*
JOHN HILBERG	Chairman of the Board John Hilberg & Sons Company Cincinnati, Ohio	*(December 7, 1971)*
JACK D. REEDER	President Dayton Coca-Cola Bottling Company Dayton, Ohio	*(December 7, 1971)*
JAMES C. BANKS	Vice President Allied Products Felker Bros. Manufacturing Co. Marshfield, Wisconsin	*(February 2, 1972)*
WALTER C. MERCER	President and Chief Executive Officer The Ohio National Bank of Columbus Columbus, Ohio	*(February 29, 1972)*
JAMES W. HOESCHLER	President Hoeschler Realty Corporation La Crosse, Wisconsin	*(April 27, 1972)*
SAM M. COHODAS	President The Miners' First National Bank & Trust Co. Ishpeming, Michigan	*(November 14, 1972)*